Fancy FEATHERED FRIENDS

Susan McKelvey

American Quilter's Society

P. O. Box 3290 • Paducah, KY 42002-3290
www.AQSquilt.com

Located in Paducah, Kentucky, the American Quilter's Society (AQS) is dedicated to promoting the accomplishments of today's quilters. Through its publications and events, AQS strives to honor today's quiltmakers and their work and to inspire future creativity and innovation in quiltmaking.

EDITOR: JANE TOWNSWICK
TECHNICAL EDITOR: HELEN SQUIRE
GRAPHIC DESIGN: LYNDA SMITH
COVER DESIGN: MICHAEL BUCKINGHAM
PHOTOGRAPHY: CHARLES R. LYNCH & RICHARD WALKER

Library of Congress Cataloging-in-Publication Data
McKelvey, Susan Richardson.
     Fancy feathered friends for quilters / By Susan McKelvey
          p.   cm.
     ISBN 1-57432-812-3
     1. Appliqué--Patterns. 2. Patchwork--Patterns. 3.
  Quilting--Patterns. 4. Birds in art. I. Title.

  TT779.M39 2003
  746.46'041--dc21   2003001437

Additional copies of this book may be ordered from the American Quilter's Society, PO Box 3290, Paducah, KY 42002-3290, or online at www.AQSquilt.com.

$\mathcal{D}$edication

To Douglas

For the support he has always given me – generously, proudly, and without complaint. We have grown up together and are growing old together. Our children blossomed under his inspiring love tempered with strength, respect, and his ever-present logic. To Douglas, then, I dedicate this book, as we move unbelievably into our fifth decade of marriage.

May bluebirds ever grace your shoulders.

Acknowledgments

I love to include birds in my quilts, and for many years I have enjoyed drafting quilt designs that feature birds in a variety of styles and tucking them into my quilts wherever possible. I have long been a collector of bluebird china and ephemera, as well as antique quilts and linens. When my collection grew to almost overwhelming proportions, it seemed time to compile my belongings into a book. The result, with the help of Barbara Smith and Helen Squire at AQS, my patient editor, Jane Townswick, and Lynda Smith, graphic designer, is this source book of bird designs and quilts, which I hope will inspire you to go beyond my vision and create singing quilts of your own.

My thanks go to all of the quilters who helped make the quilts I so blithely envisioned, and to Alison Jones Spargo, for the loan of her quilt, BLUEBIRDS OF HAPPINESS, page 12.

Contents

Introduction

Birds of all kinds, especially bluebirds, have fascinated me for many years. I delight in watching them feed outside my kitchen window and enjoy pondering their appeal, especially to quilters. Their colorful beauty accounts for much of that appeal, I suppose, and in recent years, their need for protection. The grace and delight they show in proximity to people make them the perfect symbol for happiness, domesticity, and peaceful family life. As I putter in my kitchen or sewing room, I can always cheer myself by singing lines from "Zip-A-Dee-Doo-Dah," the song Uncle Remus sang in the Walt Disney movie, *Song of the South*. I treasure the image of Uncle Remus strolling contentedly through the woods, a cartoon bluebird perched upon his shoulder, and singing cheerfully. Indeed, the sight of a beautiful bluebird still gives me the same feeling that "Everything is satisfactual!"

Many beautiful birds grace the following pages, some delicate and sweet, some chunky and stylized, some elegant and sophisticated. They represent several styles and periods of quilt history. Some were inspired by the simple shapes of folk art quilts, some by the graceful birds on quilts of the early 1900s. You can use any of these birds in any block or any quilt design you wish. Mix and match them to create new designs. Tuck them in among other flowers, vines, or vases. Enlarge or reduce them to fit your needs. Add details to simple shapes to make them more sophisticated. These fanciful feathered friends are my gift to you. Your gift to me will be to make them your own. May the bluebird of happiness sit on your shoulder and add joy and beauty to your life and your quilting.

Susan McKelvey

Chapter 1

Bird Design Inspirations

"Everything bluebird" was popular at the beginning of the twentieth century: linens, tablecloths, needlework, and even–to my absolute delight and financial ruin–quilts. In both linens and quilts, the designs were frequently embroidered and pastel, and kept to the predominant color scheme of 1910 to 1920. The motifs were precious–birds, flowers, nests, ribbons and bows, and branches.

The beautiful swooping bluebirds that we see on dinnerware also grace jewelry and dresser accessories from the period. They appear on postcards and greeting cards for all occasions.

Birds of all kinds, especially bluebirds, have appeared in art and folk art for hundreds of years. In the last two centuries, bluebirds have added their graceful presence to all decorative arts. Let's take a look at a variety of sources of bluebird designs and other bird motifs and explore the many ways they can inspire you to create beautiful birds of your own for your quilts.

China, Linens, and Decorative Arts

Some of the most delightful venues for the cheery flutter of birds have been china and textiles, which I have collected for many years. I remember my delight in the early 1980s, when I spotted my first piece of Bluebird China in an antique shop–sweet chubby, angelic bluebirds atop pink-blossomed boughs. I had never noticed that particular pattern before, but my bluebird collection began that day in that Scottville, Michigan antique shop. It was also the start of this book and the quilts it contains.

I discovered to my delight that the design on my china platter was only one of dozens made by many U.S. china manufacturers in the early 1900s; it was basic tableware designed for daily use. There are two basic design styles–one with sweet pastel birds amid pink blossoms, and the other with elegant swallows in deep cobalt blue, swooping and gliding

Vintage ephemera featuring bluebirds. Author's collection.

U.S. china from the early 1900s. Author's collection.

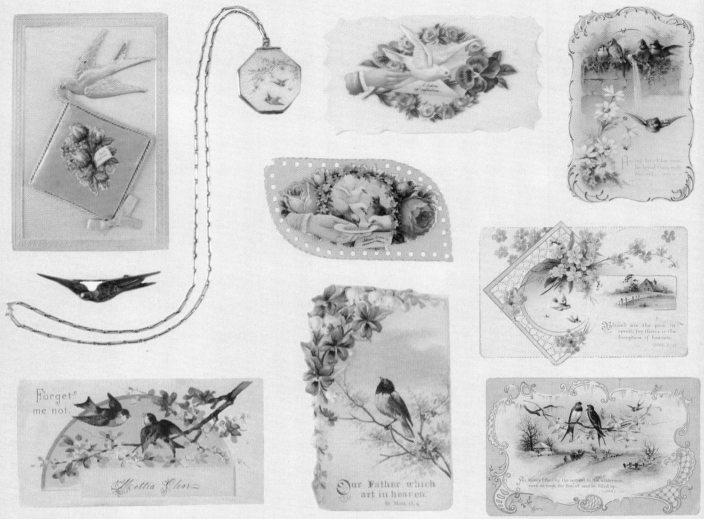

More vintage jewelry and ephemera from the author's collection.

Bavarian china from the early 1900s. Author's collection.

across plates, bowls, pitchers, and myriad accessories. Some of the swallow china is Bavarian and some American. These, too, lift my heart with their rich color and exquisite detail.

My passion for bluebird quilts began with the same sense of serendipity that started my china collection. A few years ago at the end of an auction on a hot summer's day, I stood admiring my treasures, paying little attention to the bidding still going on around me. Suddenly my attention was riveted on the auctioneer, as he pulled an appliquéd bluebird summer spread out of a box. I jumped into the bidding, but my heart immediately plummeted to my toes. Too late! Luckily, there was a mate, which I did get! Years later, I found an embroidered version of the same design. These two quilts began my bluebird quilt collection.

Popular Bluebird Designs
of the Twentieth Century

Embroidered needlework items from the author's collection.

Nineteenth and Early Twentieth Century Fabrics and Quilts

From realistic and elegant to simple and folksy, birds were important elements in nineteenth century appliqué, fabrics, and quilts. The bluebird craze of the early twentieth century was only one stage in designers' love of birds, for birds have graced fabrics and quilts since quilting began in the United States. Eighteenth and early nineteenth century fabrics featured birds of all kinds, from strutting pheasants, to eagles clutching arrows, to delicate songbirds fluttering amidst beautiful blossoms. Often these birds made their way into quilts. Women cut them out of fabrics like these and used them as appliqué elements in the *broderie perse* designs of the early 1800s.

Embroidered birds of the states quilt patterns and kits became popular in the 1920s and 1930s. The birds on these quilts were more realistic in color and shape, and included more detail than birds depicted on earlier quilts. The feedsack below, circa 1920–1930, contains a bird similar to the birds of states bird. Typically, each block on a birds of the states quilt was embroidered with the state's name and the state bird and flower.

Appliquéd birds included in nineteenth-century quilts were often simple in shape, stylized, and rather primitive, one-piece units with little thought given to realism.

Even in the elegant Baltimore album quilts of the mid-nineteenth century, birds remained stylized. Some were one-piece birds in folk art style, while others were made from fabrics featuring shading that made them look both realistic and elegant. Such birds can often be seen hovering over bouquets and vases, holding banners or

Primitive

Folk art

Elegant

envelopes, and eating from branches and vines. They were often peripheral to the main focus of the quilt designs.

By the early 1900s, embroidered quilts were popular, and on these, too, birds were favored motifs. Most of the bluebird quilts I have seen from this era are embroidered in blue thread on bright white backgrounds. Their shapes are similar to the swooping swallows on Bavarian plates and other home decorating pieces.

The quilt below, circa 1910, features the swooping swallows often seen on quilts of the time. They echo the birds on the curtain fabric beneath this quilt.

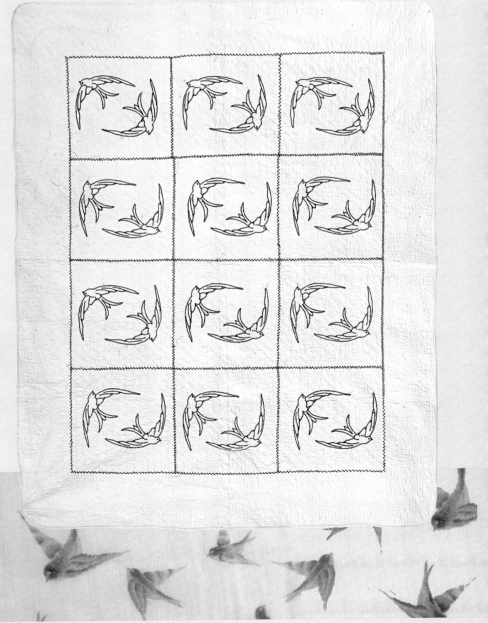

Bird Design Inspirations

Kits and patterns were popular in the early twentieth century, many of which were produced for children's quilts. Along with bunnies, dogs, kittens, and children's figures, birds (particularly bluebirds) were popular motifs. This vintage child's quilt is filled with delightful animals and graced with a bluebird border. See detail at bottom of page.

Another wonderful example of 1910 appliqué is this BASKET WITH FLOWERS & BIRDS quilt. The background is Cloth of Gold, which was a high quality, expensive fabric introduced in the early 1900s. The tiny birds, embroidered in gold thread, seem almost afterthoughts fluttering around the huge appliquéd basket and flowers.

Vintage child's quilt, BLUEBIRD OF HAPPINESS.

BASKET WITH FLOWERS & BLUEBIRDS *quilt from the authors collection.*

Fancy Feathered Friends – *Susan McKelvey*

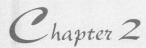

Chapter 2

Adapting Bird Designs
for Appliqué

As quiltmakers, we must think of design in simple terms, using shapes and colors in ways that will be suitable for appliqué. In other words, we need to adapt designs to the limits imposed on us by the cutting and sewing of fabric. For example, the outlines of an appliquéd bird need to look clean and crisp, as opposed to the hazy, blurred, or softened edges that can be achieved with paint. While a photograph or painting incorporates color, line, and shape, and relies heavily on detail, we must work with only color and shape.

Designs from a Single Source

To choose and adapt a design you would like from a single source, start by considering the size of the block you wish to make, the sizes of the appliqué elements you wish to include in it, and how easy those shapes will need to be stitched. For example, a flower with very detailed petals on a china plate may need to become a flower that has larger, simpler petals for appliqué. Ask yourself questions like these: How can I translate the detail of paint or pen and ink into simple outlines? How can I achieve dimension? How can I achieve shading? Let's go through the process of adapting a design for appliqué, starting with this bluebird and floral design from an early twentieth century china plate.

❏ Decide which elements of the original design you want to adapt for appliqué. For example, do you want to work with all the birds, or perhaps just a single bird? Or would you like to include some branches and flowers as well? For this adapta-

tion exercise, I have chosen to work with the little bird on the left side of the top branch and a few of the flowers, leaves, and berries. These shapes will fit nicely into the format of a square quilt block.

❏ Analyze the original elements and decide how to simplify them. Notice that the artist who created the designs on the china plate has already divided the bird into three sections: the tummy, the body, and the two wings. The branch is easy to adapt for appliqué by using bias strips. The tiny, multi-petaled blossoms and minute leaves are somewhat more difficult to adapt, because of their small size in proportion to the birds. One solution for this is to simplify the flowers, as I did, making them larger, and featuring fewer of them. Another possibility would be to stitch the flowers in silk ribbon embroidery.

❏ Gather the supplies you need for drafting your own appliqué block. You will need access to a photocopy machine, plus the following: tracing paper, graph paper, pencils and erasers, removable tape, lightbox (optional, but nice).

❏ Enlarge the original design on a photocopy machine. Lay the plate on the bed of a photocopy machine and make one copy, enlarging the design to the maximum. Continue making more photocopies, enlarging each one until you have an image that is approximately 4-6 inches. (You may need to tape quarter sections of the original design together to do this.)

❏ Trace the enlarged design onto tracing paper, including the details as they are on the original. To do this, tape the enlarged design on a flat surface or lightbox with removable tape, and tape a piece of tracing paper on top.

❏ Simplify the shapes of the original design. Tape another piece of tracing paper over your traced design, and outline the shapes in pencil, changing or deleting elements as you desire. You may find that this process takes several stages. This is the design stage—don't be afraid to play with shape, size, and details, and make several drafts! When you are satisfied with your adaptation of the original design, go over your lines with a heavy, black permanent marker, so they will be easy to see.

Look below, at my adaptation of the original design on the china plate, and notice how I have simplified and altered the size of various elements. The bird is now in four sections: the tummy, the body/head, the right wing, and the left wing. I copied a few lines from the original to suggest directional shading for the bird, and I enlarged and simplified the flowers and leaves. This gives me the option to either appliqué the petals out of one piece of fabric, or use multiple fabrics, depending on my final block size and my skill level.

❏ Enlarge your finished design as needed for your appliqué project. For this drafting exercise, I isolated one bird, but I used the entire trio of birds for BLUE BIRDS & BLOSSOMS. The pattern is included on page 43.

Techniques for Tiny Elements

Tiny elements that you don't want to enlarge or that are still small, even after enlarging, can be hard to appliqué. For things like birds' beaks and eyes, tiny leaves, and flower stamens, it can be a good idea to keep to embroidery or inking.

Designs from Different Sources

When I see designs or motifs I like on carpet or tile, embroidered linens, or print fabrics, I like to make sketches of them and add them to my file of design ideas. My BLUEBIRD MEDALLION quilt, page 45, was inspired by combining design elements from two such artifacts. The birds are based on the swooping swallows on the Bavarian china plate shown on page 8, and the circular wreath developed from the flowers on the embroidered antimacassar shown on page 9. When drawing this design, I left the inside of the wreath open for writing or exquisite quilting, and I enlarged the flowers and leaves. In my finished quilt, I defined the wreath by using two values of beige and making the outer background fabric a floral print.

Observing Copyright Law

The laws of copyright are becoming a major issue in the quilt world, and a word of caution is in order. Many designs, whether pictures, greeting cards, or patterns for sale, are copyrighted. This means that you may not use them to make a profit from the quilt you make. Pattern makers expect you to use their patterns only "for your own, one-time use." Should you ever wish to use a design for a moneymaking venture or a guild project, it is the better part of valor to ask for written permission. Adapting and altering a design (the old 10% myth) is not enough to make a design yours—it is still derivational.

Designs that pre-date 1920 are usually copyright-free. That is why we can adapt wonderful designs from antique appliqué quilts for our own quilt projects. A good rule of thumb is, "When in doubt, don't," or "When in doubt, do some research."

Chapter 3

Choosing a Fabric Palette

The great wealth of fabric available in today's marketplace offers something to suit every possible period, style, color palette, and mood. Enjoy it! Many of us old-timers remember the early days in the 1970s and early 1980s when cotton quilt fabrics were few and far between, frequently ugly, and the word *calico* meant bright flower sprigs in garish colors. Today's diverse fabrics present an opportunity to create pictorial and other special effects, and the ever-increasing variety of textile pens and inks makes it possible to add beautiful details and our own personal color touches to our quilts. Let's look at the process of selecting a fabric palette and ways to use fabrics to create special effects in a quilt.

Types of Contrast

When you audition fabrics for any project, the colors you choose and how they interact with each other is the most important consideration. Every quilt you make will benefit from contrast of some type. Include one or more of the following types of contrast to make your quilt designs both powerful and dynamic:

❏ Color Contrast

This type of contrast can be either subtle (low contrast) or vibrant (high contrast), depending upon the strength of the colors you choose. Remember that pure colors are stronger than grayed, warm, cool, dark, or light colors.

❏ Warm and Cool Colors

Using warm and cool colors together will create a vibrant, high-contrast quilt. Combine them in varying amounts to create an effective color scheme.

❏ Complementary and Triadic Colors

Complementary and triadic colors will produce vibrant, high-contrast color schemes, especially when you use them in unequal amounts.

❏ Analogous Colors

Used together, analogous colors create movement across the surface of a quilt, enabling you to direct the viewer's eye wherever you want it to go in a design.

❏ Pure Versus Dull or Grayed Colors

Adding a single bright color to an otherwise quiet color scheme adds sparkle to a quilt design and draws the viewer's eye to the pure color.

❏ Value

If there is one kind of contrast I do not see enough of in quilts, it is contrast in value. Don't be afraid to include some very dark and some very light fabrics, or use several subtly different values of a color to add interest and movement to a quilt. Many quilters tend to be attracted to medium-value fabrics, because they are often filled with beautiful patterns, and because a medium-value quilt is a "safe" quilt. Go beyond the medium! A touch of dark in a light quilt or a hint of light in a dark quilt can make a world of difference.

shade

pure color

tint

❏ Fabric Selection

Include an array of different types of fabric for greater visual interest: geometrics, florals, stripes, and solids—the more the merrier!

❏ *Print Scales*

Be sure to include a variety of print sizes in your quilt. Include a selection of large- and small-scale prints and everything in between for greatest effect.

❏ *Fabric Styles*

While contrast adds zip and sparkle to a quilt, a word also needs to be said about continuity. An effective quilt design must present visual continuity, both in style and overall mood. As you audition fabrics for your color palette, look for a sameness of fabric style, whether your preference is folksy, romantic, childlike, contemporary, or elegant.

❏ *Mood*

Before you take yourself off to the quilt shop, have a plan in mind for the way you want your quilt to look. Do you want it to be a soothing quilt for a friend, a bright quilt for a child, or a quilt with a vibrant color scheme that will be a showstopper at a quilt exhibit? Are you going to stretch yourself color-wise with this quilt, or stick to your most comfortable, familiar style? How can the fabrics you choose help you create the mood you want to portray in your quilt?

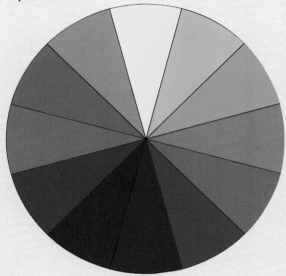

Color wheel, as seen in Color for Quilters II, *by author*

Color Selection Hints

Part of the great joy in collecting fabric and designing quilts is handling the fabric, so play, play, play! Set aside some time to fiddle with several color schemes, substitute fabrics, and rearrange them as you desire. You'll find it to be time well spent, and you'll learn more and more about color and the design process each time you experiment with fabric and color.

❏ *Small-scale Projects*

When I was learning about color, I made little quilts. That way, I could learn about a color concept (sometimes working in colors I did not necessarily like), and quickly move on to a new color lesson. Those small projects were valuable learning experiences for me, and they made great gifts for special people in my life. The receivers loved them, and I learned a lot of useful information from making them—always a win-win proposition!

❏ *Color Preferences*

Knowing color principles should help us in solving problems and in designing beautiful quilts. It is not meant to change our use of the colors we love. Color preference is personal—it is influenced by things as diverse as our skin color, our culture, and our personality needs at different periods of time in our lives. Stay true to your colors, but use color theory to use them in more interesting ways.

❏ *Time and Distance*

If you are having trouble choosing fabrics or solving a color problem, lay out your quilt on a bed or table, or hang it on a wall and leave it alone for a while. Close the door. Return at a later time and sneak up on it to see what you think. Things will pop out at you that you hadn't noticed when you were working so intently on the design. Rearrange and try again. Time and distance, both visual and mental, will help you get the perspective you need.

❏ *Visual Perspective*

Color is a long-distance illusion. Playing with pieces of fabric and a tiny block is a close-up experience. To see color instead of line, step back at least five feet from your quilt and squint at it (or take off your glasses, if you are near-sighted). This creates a lovely blur of lines and allows you to see only color. Notice which colors pop out and which ones recede. Analyze whether you have achieved what you had planned for your color scheme. Your color scheme is a combination of all its parts, and not dependent on a single fabric or print.

Emphasizing Design Elements

Before purchasing fabric for a quilt, make sure you have decided which elements of the quilt design you want to emphasize. Use the following design guidelines to achieve the effects you envision:

❏ Birds and flowers are usually the major elements in a floral appliqué design.

❏ Leaves and stems are usually secondary elements, color-wise. They are still important, however, because they help define the lovely curved shapes of a design.

❏ Background should recede visually or stay in the back.

❏ Decide whether you want sashing and/or borders to stand out or blend into the background. Size-wise, these are major elements in a quilt, so use color to control their power.

Creating Special Effects

The term "fussy-cutting" has come into favor for describing the art of cutting out desired portions of a fabric, usually small areas, to create specific effects in a quilt. It is the technique I recommend. Take time to look at fabrics for their potential for appliqué elements, and then "fussy-cut" them out of their backgrounds and use them to enhance your work. These fabric tips will help you along the path to creating unique effects in your quilts:

❏ *Look for Complete Pictorial Elements*

Look for fabrics that contain complete elements you might like to use for appliqué. An apple print may provide perfect apples—just cut them out individually (adding a seam allowance), and appliqué them as they are. Or use their beautiful shading and color gradations to create other elements in an appliqué design. Turn an apple into a heart, or fussy-cut along the sides to create flower petals.

In colorful leaf prints, the leaves can be cut out as they are (with seam allowances added) and used for appliqué.

Large, detailed prints with many overlapping elements are fertile sources of appliqué elements. Although many of the leaves are incomplete, you can use the direction of the leaves to create smaller, simpler leaves. Follow the leaf outlines, but simplify the outer edges for easy appliqué. The subtle shading in these pieces provides depth and detail to appliqued leaves.

❏ *Take Advantage of Details in Fabric*

Cut elements such as flowers, fruit, and leaves from prints. Because they are beautifully painted with details and shading, they are perfect for appliqué. This grape fabric contains individual grapes that are large enough to use as berries, and the beautiful shading is already built into them!

Choosing a Fabric Palette

❏ *Look Beyond the Literal*

Look at fabric prints for possibilities beyond what they actually depict. For example, lines in a hand-dyed or tie-dyed fabrics or in a print can suggest the feathers of a bird's wings.

Also keep your eyes peeled for pre-printed panels designed for making things like stuffed ducks, turkeys, bears, cats, and other animals. They often contain beautifully detailed feathers and fur, which you can also use in ways never intended by the manufacturers. Bodies and feathers for birds can be cut from such panels.

Many hand-dyed, tie-dyed, mottled prints, and those printed to look hand-dyed feature interesting shading and gradations in value or color. These are perfect for petals, leaves, and bird wings. The birds' tummies and the pansy petals from AMID THE PANSIES, page 62, were all "fussy-cut" from hand-dyed fabrics as seen at the top of the next column.

Using Pre-Printed Panels

Don't ignore pre-printed pictorial panels designed for pillows, household accessories, and wall quilts as possible fabric sources. Water, animal fur or feathers, the fields and mountains of a landscape—all of these can provide colors and patterns for interesting flowers and leaves. The lovely home decoration fabric shown below was a pre-printed landscape panel with an eagle in the foreground. What attracted me to it was the wonderful sky. All of the lilies and leaves shown below were cut from this same panel, and the resulting appliqué images are fabulous! The stems and stamen were inked with fabric pens. Animal prints offer fur and feather shadings that can be cut to the shapes and sizes you need.

Chapter 4

Preparing for Appliqué

After choosing a pattern and fabrics for a quilt, it is time to prepare the appliqué elements for sewing. This involves making templates and marking fabric.

❏ Photocopy the block pattern you want to use from this book, especially if you wish to combine it with other patterns or re-size it.

❏ Use a thick marker to trace the pattern onto a piece of tracing paper. The lines need to be bold enough to see easily through fabric. You will use this traced pattern to mark the background fabric and as a visual reference guide while you applique, so it does not need to be on high quality paper.

Making Templates

Start by choosing the template material you wish to work with, and follow these guidelines to make accurate, easy-to-use templates for hand appliqué:

❏ Lay the template material over the shape you wish to trace, and mark it with a pen such as the Identipen™ (page 29). Cut out the template with a pair of scissors reserved for paper and plastic, taking care to stay directly on your marked lines.

❏ For any large element or shape that is used only once, you can trace the shape from the pattern directly onto the fabric. To do this, use a lightbox or window, so that you can see through the fabric easily. Layer the fabric over the pattern, mark the turning line with a fabric pen, and cut out the shape with a ⅛" to ¼" seam allowance outside the marked line.

❏ Organize the cut appliqué elements. Store your appliqué elements in labeled plastic bags, or pin them onto a large pincushion until you need to stitch them.

Placement Marks

My minimal marking methods may be a bit unorthodox, but they are logical, easy, and accurate. I developed them as I worked, and realized how few lines one actually needs to mark: just direction and position. Try my marking methods to see if they work for you, and adapt them to your own style.

1 Cut the background fabric 4 inches larger than you want the finished block to be. This gives you plenty of room to adjust and trim the block to size later. Press horizontal, vertical, and diagonal lines on the background fabric, as shown. This provides the basic lines for centering any design. Open up the square, and press it flat, leaving the section fold lines visible.

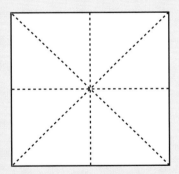

2 Pin the background fabric over your traced pattern, using a lightbox or window, if necessary. Mark the placement of appliqué elements in pencil or any marker that will not bleed, yet is easily visible on the background fabric and will remain so during the appliqué process.

3 Decide which elements define and control the design. For example, any center element or large directional element, such as stems, will control a design. These lines must be marked first and well. The simple block with a vase has three stems, three flowers, two large leaves and six small leaves (Box A, page 20).

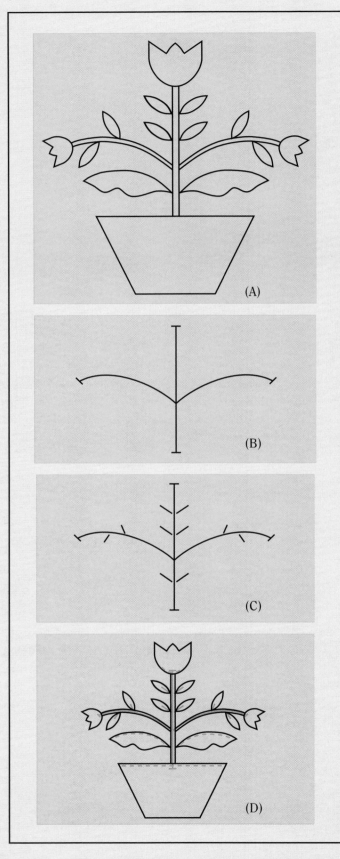

(A)

(B)

(C)

(D)

4 Mark key lines to indicate the positions of the stems. The key for stems is to follow a routine marking procedure and to follow it consistently. Mark a single key line for each stem, marking the same side of each stem each time. This will make the appliqué process easier. Mark the outer ends of each stem by stopping the marker precisely where the stem fabric should be cut (approximately ¼" beyond the point where the stem will be covered by another element, such as a flower or vase). Mark this place with a tiny crosswise line. Also mark the exact points at which any stem will meet another stem (Box B).

5 To mark the placement of a minor leaf, you only need to know two things: where it touches the stem, and the angle or direction in which it lies on the background fabric. The cut leaf tells you its outer shape and length. Just mark a key line that touches the stem at the exact point where the leaf point should touch, and go outward just far enough to show the angle for positioning the leaf on the background fabric (Box C).

6 To mark the placement of flowers, major leaves, and other important elements, you also need to know where they touch the stem and the direction or angle at which they lie on the background fabric. Rather than marking the actual positions of the shapes on the background fabric, mark key lines approximately ⅛" inside the shape's edge to be sure that the finished appliqué will cover the lines. You can mark inside the top or bottom of a shape, or any area that gives you the correct position.

7 When you finish marking key lines on the background fabric, it will look something like the block in Box D. Notice that that the stitched appliqué elements will cover and hide all of the key lines.

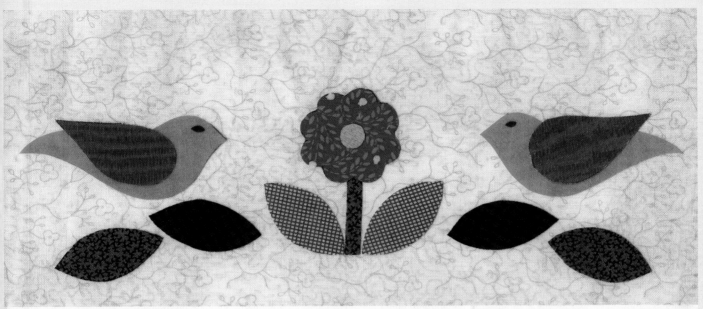

BLUE BIRDS OF HAPPINESS, *background fabric by Susan McKelvey for Benartex.*

Planning a Stitching Sequence

Stems widths can vary, depending on your design, but most patterns suggest a stem width. Delicate stems can be as narrow as ⅛", and ¼" stems are another useful width to have on hand for a wide variety of projects. Even wider stems look great on large-scale designs. Consider making a number of bias stems or vines in a variety of colors and widths. That way, you'll have a ready supply available for future projects. Store the pressed and ready-to-sew stems/vines wrapped around a large pincushion or a cardboard paper towel center.

To determine the sewing order for an appliqué design, think first about which elements overlap other elements. Then follow these guidelines:

1 First, stitch any straight center elements that define the design, such as stems, leaves, or flowers.

2 Next stitch flowers and other major elements of the block. Sew flowers before leaves, because they are the major elements, and you need to be sure there is room for them. You can always move a leaf slightly to work around a flower, but if you sew all the leaves first, you can't fudge on positioning major flowers.

3 Major leaves are the ones that, like major flowers, need to be in exact positions because they control the shape of the design. If your design contains these types of leaves, sew them on as soon as you finish stitching the stems in place.

4 Stitch small elements, such as berries, on stems, starting with the berry at the outer tip of the stem. Then add berries along the remainder of the stem. That way, you will have positioned the most important element first, and you can either eliminate or adjust the placements of other berries if there is not enough room along the stem (This frequently happens since the berries each person makes can vary in size.)

5 Minor leaves are little ones that can be moved slightly to work around major elements. Stitch these after the major elements are appliquéd.

❏ Template Materials

Here are the things I like to keep on hand for making templates to suit various kinds of appliqué. Explore the benefits of any you haven't tried before.

Tracing paper If you plan to use a template often, take the time to cut it out of template plastic. But if it will be used only once, it is easier (and cheaper) to cut it out of tracing paper, which you can see through easily and trace around once or twice without a problem.

Template plastic Sturdy as well as translucent, template plastic is good for fiddly placements on fabric. The plastic keeps its shape and doesn't wear down, which makes it ideal for templates you will use many times, such as leaves. Plastic templates for a project or a theme (like birds) are easy to store in a plastic bag for future use.

Freezer paper Freezer paper is cheap, available at any grocery store, and easy to use. Each piece can be ironed onto fabric about four times before it loses its stickiness. When you need a template you can reuse many times, you can cut a stack of identical templates at one time by folding the freezer paper, marking the top layer, and cutting all of the layers at once. When it is ironed on fabric, freezer paper makes marking appliqué turning lines easy and accurate.

Fusibles Iron-on fusibles work in the same way that freezer paper does. The explosion in the production of fusibles promises exciting options in template making. Experiment with new ones, testing for adhesiveness and ease of use.

❏ Fabric Marking Pens

Use whatever color fabric pen will show on a particular fabric. Besides the faithful #2 pencil, fabric marking pens come in light colors for dark fabrics and dark colors for light fabrics. For medium-colored and busy print fabrics, try the Pigma Micron .01mm pen in whatever color is most visible (black and brown are must-haves). For projects that will take a long time to sew (large, one-piece Hawaiian designs, for example), the Pigma pen is wonderful. It stays visible throughout the lengthy sewing process, which is a big plus.

❏ Notions

Use high quality tools for hand appliqué for easier stitching and more fun. Here are the things I recommend keeping on hand for maximum success and enjoyment:

Thread On 100% cotton fabric, I like to use 100% cotton thread. Many experienced appliqué sewers are using silk thread because it is fine and makes tiny, almost invisible stitches. Try silk thread. I prefer cotton on cotton, so that the thread and the fabric are of equal strength. Over the years, silk thread, which is stronger than cotton, may cut the fabric. I like using lightweight Mettler 60-weight thread, which hides my stitches well. Match the thread color to the color of the appliqué element as closely as you can, going darker with the thread color if you can't quite find a match. Make it a point to buy all shades of gray you can find—they blend beautifully with most medium colors.

Needles For needle-turn appliqué, I prefer long, slender needles with sharp points, because they help you to make tiny, hidden stitches. Milliners and straw needles are good choices. Sizes #11 and #12 are wonderfully slender, and they both slide through fabric layers like butter. If you can't thread them, a needle threader will help. They are so slender that they bend easily, so buy lots of them, keep them on hand, and replace as needed.

Needle threaders Many types and brands of needle threaders are widely available, varying in price and in charm. But the principle is the same; a needle-threader allows you to thread slender needles easily, and it will prove to be a useful tool as your eyes age.

Scissors Invest in two kinds of scissors: paper scissors to cut plastic and paper templates, and good fabric scissors. Appliquérs need to carry a pair of high quality, short scissors with sharp points that can clip those inside curves down to a thread from the turning line. I prefer embroidery or tailor's scissors, which have both points the same. Keep scissors protected in a leather sheath to keep your hands and your fabrics safe.

Straight pins For hand appliqué, straight pins must be slender, so they will slide easily through several layers of fabric. They also need to have sharp points, so they will not catch in the fibers of fabric. Look for silk pins with tiny heads that make it harder to tangle thread around them. Preference for length varies; some people like short sequin pins, because they are less likely to get caught on thread as you sew. I find long pins easier to grasp in my fingers. Try pins in different lengths, and stick to these three criteria: slender, sharp, and small headed.

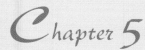

Chapter 5

Susan's Needle-turn Appliqué

Bottom Edge Appliqué

Many appliquérs stitch along the top of the appliqué shape, right-handers heading left and left-handers heading right. Think for a moment of the appliqué element with its edge folded under as a hill rising up from the flatlands of the background fabric. When you sew along the top edge, you are looking over the fold of the seam allowance. You are tucking and straightening the seam allowance with the needle in an awkward position, pointed back toward your body. As I taught myself to appliqué, I found this process not only awkward, but illogical. For that reason I began stitching along the bottom edge of the element. When you do this, the delicate turn line is visible, your hand is in an ergonomically correct position, the needle is held at a comfortable angle, and you are in position to do the most subtle adjusting of the seam allowance, points and curves. Those of you who have already perfected appliqué over the top may not see a need to change. However, if you are a beginner, I recommend you try it. You may like it.

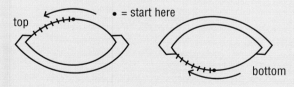

Sewing Horizontally

Always hold the appliqué element so you are sewing horizontally across your lap. This position doesn't strain your hands. Get into the habit of continually turning the appliqué piece.

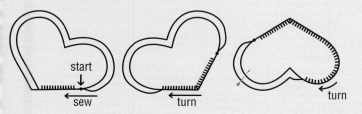

The Challenges

These are the challenges presented in some form by every appliqué piece: straight sides, inner and outer curves, and inner and outer points. Straight sides and gentle curves are easy. Sharp curves and all points are more difficult.

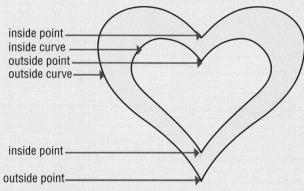

A hollow heart is the perfect shape on which to practice appliqué techniques because it contains inside and outside curves and inside and outside points. I recommend you use a heart (as shown above) as your practice piece.

The Process

The illustrations on pages 24–25 show the direction as I stitch along the base of the hill on a single heart. All techniques are the same whether you stitch along the top or along the bottom. Only the way you hold the appliqué elements changes. The position of the heart in each illustration changes to show it in the correct position for sewing across your lap.

1 *Mark the Appliqué Element.* Draw and cut out a template to mark the sewing line of your heart. Place the template on top of your fabric and mark the sewing line. Cut out the heart with a ⅛" seam allowance on each side. Don't clip anywhere yet.

2 *Pin the Element in Place.* Being a lazy quilter, I pin rather than baste. Most appliqué elements are small and can be sewn quickly, so a few pins will hold them until they are sewn. Pin the heart to the background fabric. Place the pins at key points perpendicular to the outside edges, catching the outer edge with the first prick to anchor it. Pinning parallel to the edge or just in the center can cause distortion.

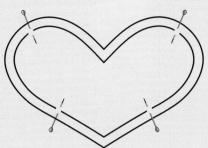

3 *Begin at the Straightest Place.* Pin along the easiest place to start—on the side, heading toward the point at the bottom of the heart. Fold and pin the seam allowance under on the turn line, pinning all the way to the point.

4 Bring the threaded needle through from the back of the background fabric to begin and take *tiny stitches*, as close together as you can, catching just a thread or two into the folded edge. As you stitch, give a gentle tug every so often to hide stitches in the fibers of the fabric.

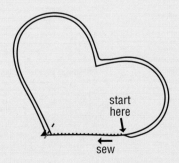

5 The trick to a perfect *outer point* is to ignore the second side of the point until after you have finished the first side. Stitch all the way to just inside the point and take a double stitch precisely at that point to anchor it.

With the point anchored, you can fiddle with the point. First, set up the second side of the heart by pinning the seam

allowance under with one pin about an inch ahead. With this pin in place, look at the fabric tag sticking out from the point. If it is a large tag, clip parallel to the length of the heart to remove bulk. If it is a small tag, you can tuck it under without clipping. Never clip the fragile ⅛" allowance.

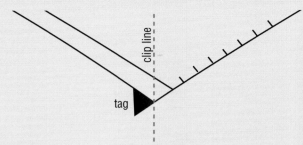

6 *Turn you work* so the heart is upside down, and use the needle tip to catch the seam allowance and pull it under and toward you. Use your opposite thumb to finger-press the turned point in place.

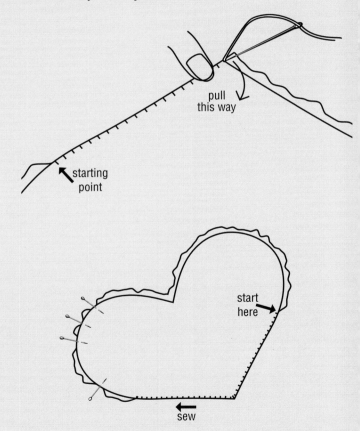

Turn the heart into position to sew the second side.

7 To ease in the fabric along the curve at the top of the heart, closely pin the curve in place ahead of your sewing. You can *ease the fabric* under between the pins.

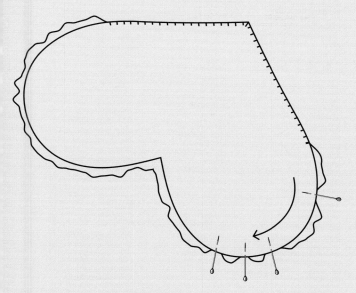

8 Continue stitching until you can not stitch without *clipping* the inner point. Make one clean cut all the way into the marked line so you can turn it under and hide the line.

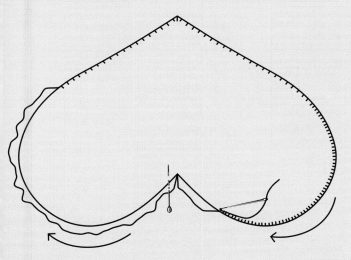

9 To hold the other curve in place while you fiddle with the *inner point*, place a pin on the opposite side of the clip, parallel and as close as possible to the clip. Weave the pin in

and out of the fabric several times to hold the fabric in place. Slide the allowance under with one sweep of the side of the needle, then push and pull with the needle point to hide the threads. Take many stitches close together within ¼" of the inside point and take several stitches at the exact point.

Pin the curve of the second side and turn the second side of the inner point under, and sew it. Finish sewing the heart.

The Inside of the Heart

The inside of the heart contains an inside point, outside point, and inside curves. You will need to clip at the inside point and along the inside curves.

I generally dislike rules, but I designed the following two rules for myself through trial and error. You may find them useful:

Never clip unless you have to.

If you have to clip, do it at the last possible second and clip as little as possible.

Begin sewing on the easiest part of the heart, the straight side, heading toward the inside point. Treat it just as you did the first inside point; clip the point just before you reach it and ease the fabric under with the needle.

Chapter 6

Embellishing Fabric with Ink

Many of the quilts in this book are embellished with ink. On some, inking is used to sign a block in the traditional manner, but it is also used in many other interesting ways. On some quilts, I added a poem. On others, I used ink to add details or create pictorial effects. This chapter will help you explore some of the many ways that inking can help you enhance your quilts.

Inking Options

Here are some of my favorite ways to ink fabrics for a quilt.

Enjoy any techniques you may already be familiar with and experiment with others that are new to you.

❏ Adding Signatures to Blocks

One of the most common ways to add inking to a block is by signing it. In my SWIRLING BLUEBIRDS quilt (page 81), the corner of each block is signed in traditional mid-nineteenth century style, with the signature embellished with lovely little Victorian designs. Here the beautiful designs are traced (see Resources on page 110) and the names are added freehand.

An easy and effective way to add a signature to a quilt block is to wrap the name around an element in it.

Detail from Birds of Old, *Block #9 - Cherry Pickers, pages 106-107*

This looks especially nice along a curve, such as the tree trunk in the Cherry Pickers block by Georgina Shultz, or when tucked into the curve of the vase in the Vase of Plenty block by Linda Tonyes.

Detail from Birds of Old, *Block #5 - Vase of Plenty, pages 100-101.*

Inking Supplies

❏ *Removable Magic Tape by 3M®*

You will enjoy using this tape because it does not ruin paper or fabric, peels off easily, and can be re-used several times.

❏ *Lightbox or Light Table*

There are many reasonably priced lightboxes on the market today, and I highly recommend one for any quilter. They are especially useful for drafting and creating your own appliqué patterns. You can make your own lightbox by placing a table lamp between two stacks of books and putting a piece of glass or Plexiglas over the books.

❏ *Tracing Paper*

For designing and altering patterns, tracing paper is a must-have. Buy a pad or a large roll of tracing paper at an art supply shop or an office supply store.

❏ *Fabrics*

Smooth 100% cotton fabrics work best with fabric pens; you're likely to have a ready supply of suitable fabrics in your stash.

❏ *Pens for Writing on Fabric*

Pens suitable for writing on fabric include the following brands: the Pigma Micron™, the Identipen™, the Fabricmate™, the Fabrico™, and the Fantastics™.

❑ Incorporate Inked Words and Details

In this detail from BIRDS ON BANNERS (page 34), I have gone a step further and used inking to create large, dramatic signature spaces, which are part of the block design. Each block contains an appliquéd bird perched on an inked banner. The banner could also have been appliquéd, but I wanted to demonstrate how easy and how much fun it is to incorporate a large inked element into an appliqué design.

Detail from DESCENDING DOVES *quilt*

Detail of inked banner from a BIRDS ON BANNERS *block*

❑ Inking the Center Area of a Medallion

My DESCENDING DOVES quilt (page 77) contains a large, open center space that cried out for either wonderful quilting or some elaborate inking. I chose to ink a lovely phrase from an antique valentine in my collection and wrote it in a scale large enough to hold its own when surrounded by the colorful birds and roses. To do this type of large inking, first trace the design or words, and then fill in with the same pen (see page 35 for more information on this technique). Here, I have left two lines just as they were first traced, so you can see the tracing process. The scroll was also traced and filled in.

❑ Adding Details to Appliqué Elements

In this AMID THE PANSIES quilt (page 62), I used a beautiful many-colored fabric for the pansy petals. Then I inked the delicate black shading around the flower centers and added green veins to the leaves.

Detail from AMID THE PANSIES *quilt*

Pen Characteristics

❏ *Pigma Micron™ Pens*

Pigma Micron pens come in fifteen colors and several sizes. I like the .01mm and .05mm sizes for writing and drawing. In addition, the brush-tip pens produce intense color and are useful for coloring solid areas and doing large-scale drawing and writing. These pens are archival, which means that the ink is non-acidic and will not erode paper or fabric over time. They also have a very slow ink flow, which allows you to write or draw easily and slowly. The tiny points allow you to write in the delicate, spidery style of nineteenth-century copperplate script, as well as in the tiny-size script found on signed antique quilts. To write well, you must learn to move the pen lightly and slowly, so that it will not catch in the woven fibers of the fabric. Pigma pens do not usually bleed much on 100% cotton fabric.

❏ *Identipens™*

These dual-tipped pens come in eight colors. The smaller point is larger than the largest Pigma point, and the large point is very thick. The ink is actually designed for writing on hard, smooth surfaces, such as glass and plastic, on which it dries instantly. This makes Identipens wonderful for drawing on template plastic or marking plastic bags in which you wish to store pens and templates. These are permanent pens but not archival. I like to use Identipens for writing very large script (¾" to 1" or higher). The large point is the perfect size to make patterns visible through paper or fabric. I often use the yellow one as a base color when shading flower petals or imitating a gold metallic look.

❏ *Fabricmate™, Fabrico™ and Fantastic™ Pens*

These pens are designed for use on fabric, and they are good for shading. They work best on a scale much larger than Pigma pens, and they are available in an extensive ranges of colors. Fabricmate and Fabrico pens each have dual points (one brush and one sharp), while the Fantastic pens are tiny disposable pens you dip into individual bottles of ink that comes in a wide variety of colors. These pens make drawing and shading on fabric easy, and you can create beautiful watercolor effects with all of them.

Inking Requirements

❏ *Purchase Fabric Pens*

It's a good idea to experiment with many different fabric pens. The brands listed here are widely available in craft stores and art supply stores, and more are being introduced as the demand increases. Try as many of them as you can, keeping in mind that any ink you use should remain permanent through multiple washings, as well as after it has been exposed to sunlight. There should not be any bleeding on the fabric as you write, and the ink should not damage the fabric over time.

❏ *Test the Fabric for Bleeding*

Always make it a point to pretest each pen for bleeding on scrap pieces of the actual fabrics you plan to use in your quilt, because every fabric is different in regard to how much ink it will absorb. Simply hold the pen upright while it touches the fabric and watch whether and how fast the ink bleeds. If bleeding occurs, it does not necessarily mean that you shouldn't use the pen, but it does mean that you will need to move the pen quickly enough across the surface of the fabric to stay ahead of the bleeding.

❏ *Heat-set the Ink*

After you finish inking a piece of fabric, heat-set the ink with a dry iron. The directions that come with the pen usually say heat-set, but what they actually mean is dry heat-set to eliminate all the moisture by either ironing the fabric or tossing it into a dryer on cotton setting.

❏ *Test the Ink for Permanence*

After heat-setting the fabric, test the inked scrap for permanence. Wait twenty four hours before testing. To do this, wash the fabric gently, using mild soap in cold water, just as you would a fine quilt. If any bleeding or discoloration occurs at this point, consider using another fabric or a different pen.

Choosing Fabrics for Inking

You can write on any fabric on which ink will show. For best results, use high quality, smoothly woven, 100% cotton fabric so that the pens will not catch on the nubbiness of the weave. Do not limit yourself to plain white or muslin, consider both solid colors and prints. Pale colors make lovely backgrounds for writing, and delicate prints fill an open background space nicely while still allowing ink to be easily visible. For more examples of fabrics like the ones shown here, look at the AMID THE HOLLY quilt on page 66, and the DESCENDING DOVES quilt on page 77.

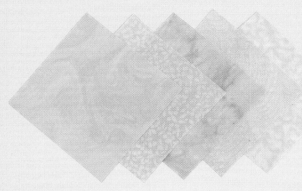

Avoid white-on-white pigment prints. These are fabrics with tiny designs painted on the top surface. Fabric inks are dyes that are absorbed into the fabric, but the pigment paint of a white-on-white fabric will block penetration of the ink. Also, the pigment paint may chip off eventually, destroying inked designs or script.

Fabric Preparation

Before you even test fabrics for inking, prepare them as you would for a quilt.

1 Pre-wash the fabric to get rid of the sizing which acts as a barrier to ink penetration.

2 Iron the fabric to promote smooth writing.

3 Pretest the pen you wish to use on the fabric, adjusting your speed and hand pressure, as needed, to avoid bleeding and facilitate smoothness of writing.

4 Stabilize the fabric, either by laying it over another piece of fabric (fast and easy), or by ironing it onto a piece of freezer paper (good for larger projects). I prefer making a workboard for a writing and drawing surface. To do this, cut a 16" square of smooth muslin and wrap it tightly around a 12" square of foam core board (available at any craft store). Tape the fabric on the back side with masking tape. This provides a lightweight and easy-to-maneuver workboard. When you lay cotton fabric on top of the cotton surface of the workboard, it does not slip.

5 After you practice inking the fabric, heat-set the ink with dry heat by ironing the fabric with a dry iron on the cotton setting or tossing it into a dryer.

Shading with Pigma™ Pens

To shade with a Pigma pen, you must hold the pen low on its side, so that you are actually using the side of the pen. Yes, even this tiny pen point has a side, and by using this side, you can shade exquisite, tiny designs on fabric.

You are aiming to create "fuzz," which is a technical term I coined for shading. To achieve this delicate look, don't hurry the process. Handle your pen with a light touch, holding it on its side until you get the feeling of how to make the fuzz as shown on the left side of the top banner on page 31. Do not draw lines as shown on the right side of the top banner. These banners show the progressive shading of the folds.

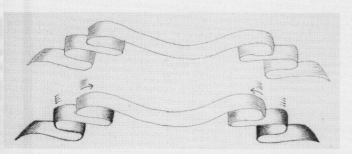

like an eyelash. It can be short or long. To darken the fuzz gradually, as shown on the outer curves of the lower banner in the photo, go over it several times with the same eyelash stroke.

1 Place the traced banner over the workboard to stabilize it while you shade in the area at the left side of the uppermost curve. To shade, always work from the outline of the banner into the center, open area (see arrows). The first time you touch the fabric will always be your heaviest touch, so begin at that line and pull lightly away from it with a short stroke of the pen.

2 After you have a light coating of fuzz in place, soften the transition from outline to shading. Beginning at the outline, use a short, light stroke, lifting the pen off the fabric at the end of every stroke. The resulting stroke looks

3 Now cover the edge of the shading with many of these eyelash strokes, until the outline blurs from shading into open space. This transition from outline to shading to open space should be gradual, as shown on the lower curves of the banner.

Helpful Tips for Shading

❑ Pigma pens will enable you to do delicate shading on a small scale; the .01mm (small) and the .05mm (large) sizes will work well for shading.

❑ Remember that you are not filling in the entire space, just shading corners and curves and leaving open space in which to write. Create a strong, but gradual, dark-light contrast. Where and how you shade will establish your personal style.

An Inking and Shading Exercise

Use the banner design below and a Pigma pen for some easy practice in tracing and shading techniques. Again, it's a good idea to try out these techniques on a scrap of the actual fabric you wish to use in a quilt before attempting a final drawing.

1 Photocopy the banner design and darken the lines to make them easier to see through fabric. Tape the design on a lightbox or to a window with removable tape.

2 Lay your fabric over the taped design and secure it in place with removable tape, or use straight pins if working with a large piece of fabric.

3 Notice that the banner design contains the outline of the banner as well as smaller lines suggesting areas to shade. First, trace *only* the banner outline. Use a Pigma pen in the same color you wish to use later for shading. Fabric over paper, even if well-anchored, can still slip, distorting the drawing, so use a light touch. If the fabric pulls, you are pressing too hard. Draw firm, even lines rather than many short, sketchy lines.

4 When you are finished tracing the outline of the banner, remove the tape. Lift the fabric from the paper, and lay it over the fabric-covered workboard. Do the rest of your inking on the workboard.

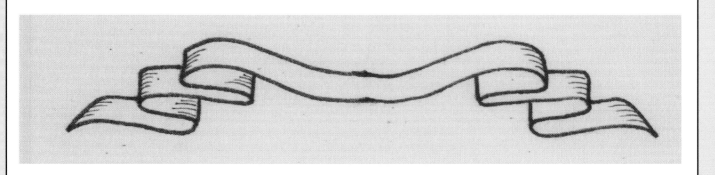

Flowers and Leaves

Practice the tracing and shading techniques shown here, using the pens listed on page 29. This should be done before beginning any major project.

☐ *Daisy Petals*

Inking your own flowers allows you to control their size, color, and shape. Enjoy using these techniques to create an original flower that is all your own.

The daisies in my HUDDLED ON A GARDEN WALL quilt shown on page 68 are cut from a solid white fabric and are very simple in shape. To give them more life and detail, I enhanced the petals with ink. You can create the same effect in your daisies by using a large pen (Identipen™, Fabrico™, or Fabricmate™) for the yellow and green shaded areas and Pigma .01mm pens in brown and green for the outlines and delicate shading.

Detail from HUDDLED ON A GARDEN WALL *quilt, page 68*

1 Trace the outline of this daisy on your chosen fabric, using a Pigma .01mm pen in the color you will use for shading (in this case, brown). The Pigma pen is perfect for tracing the turning edge of an appliqué shape because it makes a thin line that can easily be hidden during the stitching process.

2 To add depth, darken one side only, or about half of the outline on each petal. Use the yellow pen to add color on each petal, radiating out from the flower center. Darken the outline of the flower center with the green Pigma pen, and shade in the outer area with the larger green pen.

3 Use the brown Pigma pen to shade both ends of each petal, covering only some of the yellow. Include some delicate lines.

Note: For this exercise, I have inked all of the petals at the same time, to show the shading progression, but you can ink and appliqué each petal separately for a more dramatic look.

☐ Other Flower Petals

Choose a pretty pink or rose fabric to practice shading on other types of petals. Follow steps 1 through 6 using Pigma rose and blue, .01mm or .05mm pens, to ink this delicate flower.

1. With the rose pen, trace the outlines of the petals.
2. Darken part of or all the outline of each petal in varying intensity.
3. Shade with fuzz or delicate lines on each petal, radiating out from the center and inward from the tips.
4. Add a touch of blue shading.
5. Continue to darken the shading. It's a good idea to always leave some of the fabric showing.
6. Build up the shading and the resulting color until it has a rich texture.

☐ Detail to Leaves

It's easy to add veins to leaves; just draw squiggly, irregular lines in approximate positions. They need not be botanically accurate. The right leaf shows a solid fabric enhanced with inked veins, and the left leaf is an already leafy-looking fabric with inked veins.

 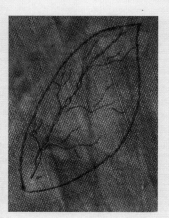

☐ Rosebuds and Calyxes

Just a little bit of ink can enhance an already lovely flower. For this rosebud I chose a marbled fabric for the bud, cutting it so that the marbling would curl around in imitation of a closed rosebud. Still not satisfied and knowing that I could enhance the illusion of the rolled bud even more, I added dark shading with a rose Pigma pen. On the tiny calyx, I added inked details after appliquéing it because the plain green seemed too stark.

Birds' Wings and Feathers

Rarely do you find the perfect fabric for appliquéd birds' wings, so it is fun to search for fabrics that can be inked to create the look of wings and feathers. Below is a blue fabric with color gradations. To create the illusion of a bird's wing and feathers:

1. Trace the wing shape on the wing-like fabric.
2. Ink in some feather lines and darken them.
3. Add shading and darken the lines.

BIRDS ON BANNERS *designed by Susan McKelvey; blocks made by quiltmakers (see page 109). Each of the nine blocks contains the same bird and banner, done in different fabrics and surrounded by different flowers and leaves. This quilt features a traditional sashing, for which I used a soft loden-green to divide the blocks without taking over the quilt. The border is also a subdued green, yet it provides a strong contrast in value to the lighter sashing. The overall mood of the quilt is peaceful, an effect created and controlled by color.*

Writing on Fabric

At the very least, we should all sign and date our quilts, leaving future historians the background information that was not left for us on many antique quilts. Better yet, we should sew labels on the backs of our quilts, which can hold lots of valuable information. If you appliqué a label on the back of a quilt, do so before you sandwich the three layers together. That way, you can quilt the label right into your quilt and make it more permanent.

If you are adding your signature to a block, you can sign it anywhere you like. Hide your name modestly in the curve of a flower or leaf, or place it proudly in an open space on the background. Make it large and bold or tiny and delicate–this is as much a matter of your style as are your quilt design and color choices. All of the writing on the quilts in this book has been done with one of two pens; the small writing with the Pigma .01mm pen and the large writing with the Identipen™. The following tips for writing on fabric will help you give your personal touch to every quilt you make.

❏ Write on the background before you appliqué. If you make a mistake, you will only have lost a piece of background fabric, rather than a completely appliquéd block.

❏ When you need to write script that measures ¾" high or higher, you can write it freehand, or trace it, using a lightbox.

❏ In my DESCENDING DOVES quilt shown on page 77, I have left some of the letters in the first-trace stage to show you how to trace and fill in. The decorative swirl at the bottom was also traced and filled in later.

Embellishing Fabric with Ink

Writing Small

1 Choose the poem, phrase, or other information you want to write on fabric. Write it out on a piece of lined paper as you want it to appear on your quilt. Keep the paper beside you.

2 Look at the fabric and decide the size and shape of the actual space in which you will write on the fabric.

3 Lay a piece of tracing paper over the chosen space on the fabric, and trace the outline of the space. Trace several outlines; these will function as rough drafts.

4 Draw horizontal lines ¼" apart on the rough drafts. These lines will help keep the writing straight.

5 Practice writing your message on successive rough drafts, adjusting the size and spacing of your letters and words, as necessary.

6 When you are satisfied with the draft of your message, lay it near you and use it as a guide while you write directly on the fabric.

7 If you are afraid to write on an actual quilt block after you have spent hours appliquéing it, consider writing on the background fabric *before* you begin to appliqué. This is a safe way to be sure your writing will be equal to your stitching. If you make a mistake, you will only have lost a piece of background fabric, rather than a completely appliquéd block.

Writing Large (For script ¾" or higher)

1 Choose the poem, phrase, or other information you wish to write. Write it out on a piece of paper, and keep the paper beside you.

2 Measure the space in which you wish to write.

3 On a computer, choose a type style (font) you like, and type out the words, centering them on the page. Enlarge the words to the size you think might fit your space, and print out one copy.

4 Lay the fabric over the typed words and check the spacing of the words. If necessary, return to the computer and adjust the type size. You can also use a photocopy machine to enlarge the words more than a computer will allow.

5 Tape the paper on top of a lightbox, and tape or pin the fabric over the paper. Trace only the outlines of the letters.

6 Remove the fabric from the lightbox and lay it on top of another piece of cotton fabric to stabilize it.

7 Fill in and/or shade the letters as desired. Remember that you can also do this type of writing before you appliqué.

Fitting Words into a Defined Space

To write inside a banner or any other defined, curving space, you will need to adjust the letters into a meandering curve, following these steps. You can use this method to write in any oddly-shaped area.

1 Place a piece of tracing paper over the banner design you choose and trace the outline only. Do several tracings; these will be your rough drafts.

2 On each rough draft, use a pencil to mark a vertical line indicating the center of the space, and add another line just inside the curved lower edge of the banner. You will write on this line, not on the banner outline.

3 Practice writing your message on several of your rough drafts to get the spacing right.

4 When you have the size and spacing of the words the way you like, go over your lines with a thick pen to make them more visible. Layer the fabric over your final draft, and pin it in place. Trace the banner and the words. If you are working on a very small piece of fabric, you can lay the final draft beside you and write the words freehand following the guidelines.

Actual pattern for the basic bird shape (as seen on page 34). Add seam allowances.

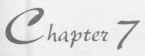

Chapter 7

Making the Quilts

How the Patterns are Organized

Because of their sizes, some of the blocks in this book are presented on several pages. Use the following guidelines as you prepare each pattern for appliqué.

❒ Each block section is named and numbered.

❒ Block sections are placed in order from left to right.

❒ The center of each block is marked with a crosshatch.

❒ The sewing sequence is presented with each block.

❒ Fabric and color ideas and stitching sequence, along with block size and finished measurements are given.

❒ The color choices are given as a starting point for choosing the colors for your own block or quilt.

Transferring Patterns onto Paper

To copy a block, start with freezer paper or tracing paper and a heavy black marker and follow these steps:

1 Cut a square of freezer paper or tracing paper slightly larger than the finished dimensions for the block you wish to make.

2 Lay the paper over the first pattern section and tape it in place with removable tape.

3 Using a heavy black marker, mark all of the pattern lines, including the center crosshatch mark, the lines of the design, the outer edges of the block, and any directions indicated on the pattern.

4 Match the center of the next pattern section to the edge of the traced first section and mark the second section in the same manner. Mark the remaining pattern sections in the same way.

Note: Some patterns are symmetrical. To make templates trace one side of the design only, and flip the paper over to transfer the key lines to your background. Doing this will ensure that both sides of the design are identical. If you wish to make a full pattern of a symmetrical block, trace one side of the block, fold the paper in half, and trace the second side from your drawn first side. That way, any slight changes you made as you traced the first half will apply to both sides of the design.

Using the Pattern Instructions

Each of the blocks that follows comes from one of the quilts in the book. Each pattern features an instruction page that will help you create your own beautiful bird blocks. Read through the Fabric and Color Ideas to discover how fabrics were used in that block, and follow the Stitching Sequence to appliqué the elements of each design in place. You can use these blocks to make any kind of project you like, in any size you desire, from pillows or single-block wall quilts, to table runners, repeat-block quilts, or album quilts Enjoy!

Rarely do I plan an entire quilt before I begin to make it. Rather, I like to begin with a concept, a mood, or a style and let the blocks speak to me as I work on them, envisioning in my mind how they need to be set together. The quilts in this book represent a variety of set and border possibilities and color schemes, while remaining true to my own style and vision. Enjoy using the following tips, set and border ideas, and ways to add your personal touch to the binding of a quilt.

Finishing Touches

❒ *Echoing the Appliqué Elements* We can get endless inspiration for beautiful borders from antique quilts, such as the Baltimore album quilts of the 1850s. Often, these quilts featured borders made of the same background fabric as the blocks, and featured decorative edges on either side. I frequently add these edgings to borders, as in the AMID THE HOLLY quilt on page 66. Notice how the color of the dogtooth edging picks up blues of the birds. For other examples of border treatments, see SPRING PUSSY WILLOW on page 48, WEDDING BOUQUET on page 52, and BIRDS OF OLD on page 93.

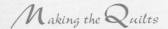

In LESLIE'S WEDDING QUILT, shown on page 108, the elaborate inner border of bluebirds and bouquets is a main design feature of the quilt center. The dogtooth border sets it off effectively from the center medallion and the outer corners. To draft traditional dogtooth edges, I made my own ruler from template plastic. After testing it out on Leslie's quilt, I realized how well it worked for fancy appliqué edges, so I designed the ruler for appliquérs everywhere to enjoy. For information on ordering this ruler, see Resources, page 110.

A lovely and effective way to tie a border and quilt center together is to repeat some of the center appliqué elements in the border, a popular style seen in many antique Baltimore quilts. I call this repetition "echoing." If you use the same amounts of a color or design in the border as you do in the quilt center, the border will become visually as important — or more important—than the center. The goal is to tie the two together without overwhelming the center (and theoretically more important) elements. Pick up elements you want to emphasize and repeat them in small ways or echoes in the border. Examine the center of your quilt to decide which elements you wish to repeat. Consider repeating the ones you think prettiest, and look for large ones, as well, to fill the border corner areas. Look for colors and fabrics that bear repeating in the border. For each technique discussed below, take time to analyze the quilts in this book, and determine which ones are used in each.

Make an undulating vine that wraps around the entire quilt, and cover it with a selection of flowers, leaves, and birds in the quilt center. Repeat the fabrics as well. This will tie the border to the center of your quilt. This vine can go in any or all directions. You can place a vine around the entire border in one direction (A), or start the vine from a bottom center motif and bring it up on both sides to meet at the top center (B). Or you can place the vine around three sides of the border, with an open area for other motifs at the top center area (C).

❑ *Echoing a Color* The vibrant purples and blues in the DESCENDING DOVES wall quilt, shown on page 77, set off the reds and yellows of the roses. Simple in composition—just a block and a border—it relies on color to provide its lush feeling. The marbled background fabric of the block adds texture to the open space, while it is light enough to ink easily. The roses and leaves from the quilt center are carried out onto two of the border corners, trailing slightly along the sides and tying the center and border together.

If the quilt center contains too little of a color that you would like to emphasize, try echoing that color in the border or binding for emphasis. This repetition will enhance the color and carry the viewer's eyes across the quilt. In HUDDLED ON A GARDEN WALL, shown on page 68, the main elements are the birds. Because they are blue and small, they do not stand out as well as the bright daisies and large brown area of the wall; by carrying out the blue and the green to the border, the birds become more prominent.

❏ *Using a Large Print* Large "prints" were often used in nineteenth-century quilts. These prints were so beautiful that they not only served as a frame for the center area of a quilt, but added elaborate pictorial designs around the edges. See BLUE BIRDS & BLOSSOMS on page 42.

❏ *Using Stripes* Stripes are wonderfully versatile fabrics for borders. Used traditionally, they create a picture frame effect. Try going beyond the traditional, and use them to create other wonderful effects from classic to contemporary. Look at HUDDLED ON A GARDEN WALL on page 68, PRETTY PAPERCUT on page 90, and BIRDS OF OLD on page 93.

❏ *Repeating a Strong Color* If a color in the center of the quilt is too strong, dilute it by repeating it somewhere in the border. This will draw the viewer's eyes across the quilt. Color play is the focus in the folksy OH, WHAT A LOVELY MEAL! quilt shown on page 72. Vivid colors and bold prints go beyond the traditional, adding zest to its design. The dark maroon background of the center on-point block makes the bright berries and checkered birds jump off the quilt, while hot oranges, bright yellows, and an orange check in the narrow border set the block off strikingly against the darker turquoise of the outer corners. To balance the quilt, the maroon of the center background area is echoed in the corner squares of the outer border and in the binding. Notice how the deep, dark color on the binding holds in the warm borders.

❏ *Borders and Bindings* My cardinal rule in designing quilt borders is: do not introduce anything new in the borders or the binding. Instead, tie the borders and binding to the quilt center in color, design, and/or style.

The binding can be the *piece de resistance* of a quilt—frosting on your cake. A tiny echo of a color you want to emphasize from the body of your quilt is often the perfect finishing touch that makes a quilt look complete. Look at each of the quilts throughout this book and notice the colors used in the bindings.

In CHEERY CHERRY TIME shown on page 54, a single border detail inspired by the border of an 1800s quilt becomes a quilt center in its own right. Bright yellows and blues enhance the traditional red and green color scheme, while the simple white background and inner border harken back to the mid-nineteenth century. The rich red narrow border outlines the center block. All four corners of the white outer border echo the cherry clusters and hearts from the quilt center. Double crosshatch background quilting sets off, but does not detract from, the traditional flavor of the piece. The red and green striped binding ties everything together without introducing any new elements.

Directional print fabrics, such as checks, plaids and stripes, can be cut on the bias to produce a touch of movement around the outer edge of a quilt, as in the red and green striped binding on this CHEERY CHERRY TIME quilt.

The ARBOR FEAST design, shown on page 57, is so elaborate and lovely that I thought it should stand alone as a wall quilt design. To set it off, a narrow purple inner border echoes the colors of the grapes, while the outer border returns to the white background. The trailing vines are echoed in only two corners of the outer border, trailing blithely along the sides. Notice that the border designs are actually larger than the center ones; without these, the center medallion would have seemed lost. Grape clusters from the appliqué design are used as quilting elements in the corners of the blocks and the outer border.

BLUE BIRDS & BLOSSOMS

SPRING PUSSY WILLOW

BLUEBIRD MEDALLION

Easy Projects

Easy Projects

WEDDING BOUQUET

CHEERY CHERRY TIME

ARBOR FEAST

Design dimensions: 17" x 20"
Block size: 25" x 25"
Finished quilt size: 34" x 34"

Blue Birds
&
Blossoms

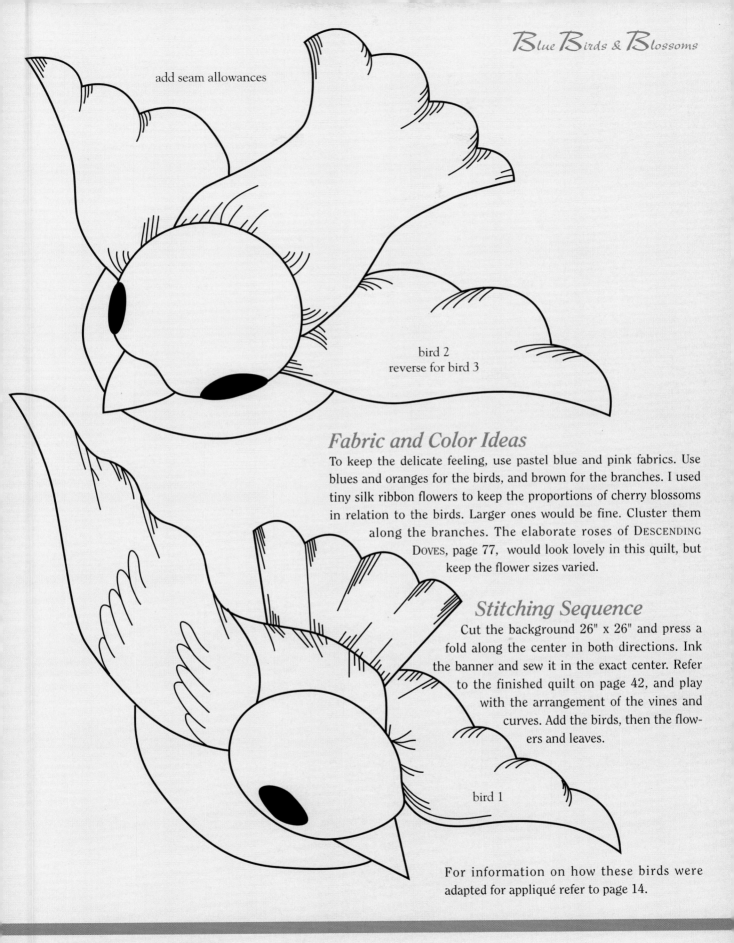

add seam allowances

bird 2
reverse for bird 3

Fabric and Color Ideas

To keep the delicate feeling, use pastel blue and pink fabrics. Use blues and oranges for the birds, and brown for the branches. I used tiny silk ribbon flowers to keep the proportions of cherry blossoms in relation to the birds. Larger ones would be fine. Cluster them along the branches. The elaborate roses of DESCENDING DOVES, page 77, would look lovely in this quilt, but keep the flower sizes varied.

Stitching Sequence

Cut the background 26" x 26" and press a fold along the center in both directions. Ink the banner and sew it in the exact center. Refer to the finished quilt on page 42, and play with the arrangement of the vines and curves. Add the birds, then the flowers and leaves.

bird 1

For information on how these birds were adapted for appliqué refer to page 14.

Detail: Silk ribbon cherry blossoms

Border Design When there is already a lot going on in the body of a quilt, you can blend the binding into the border to avoid marring the composition of the quilt, as in BLUE BIRDS & BLOSSOMS on page 42. The border fabric is already a large, busy print, so I made the binding from the same fabric.

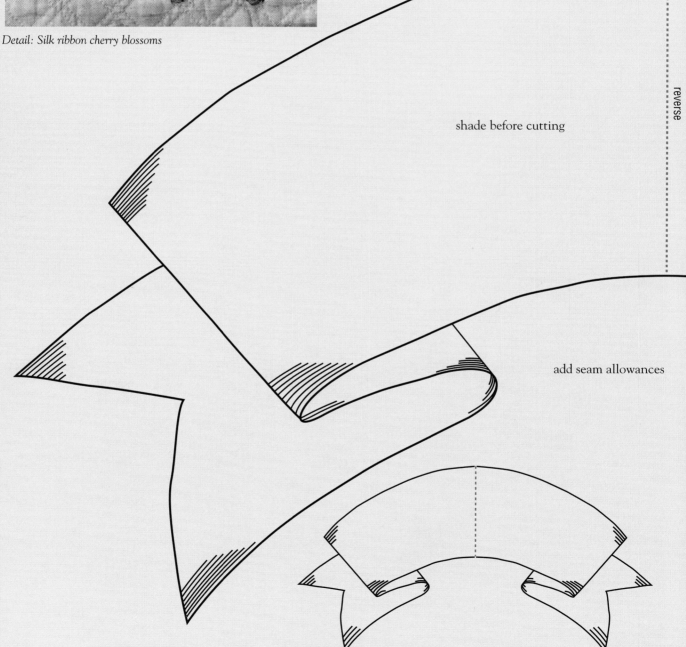

shade before cutting

reverse

add seam allowances

The woods would
be very silent
if no birds
sang there except
those who
sang best

John James Audubon

Design dimensions: 16" x 14"
Block size: 24" x 24"
Finished quilt size: 34" x 34"

Bluebird Medallion

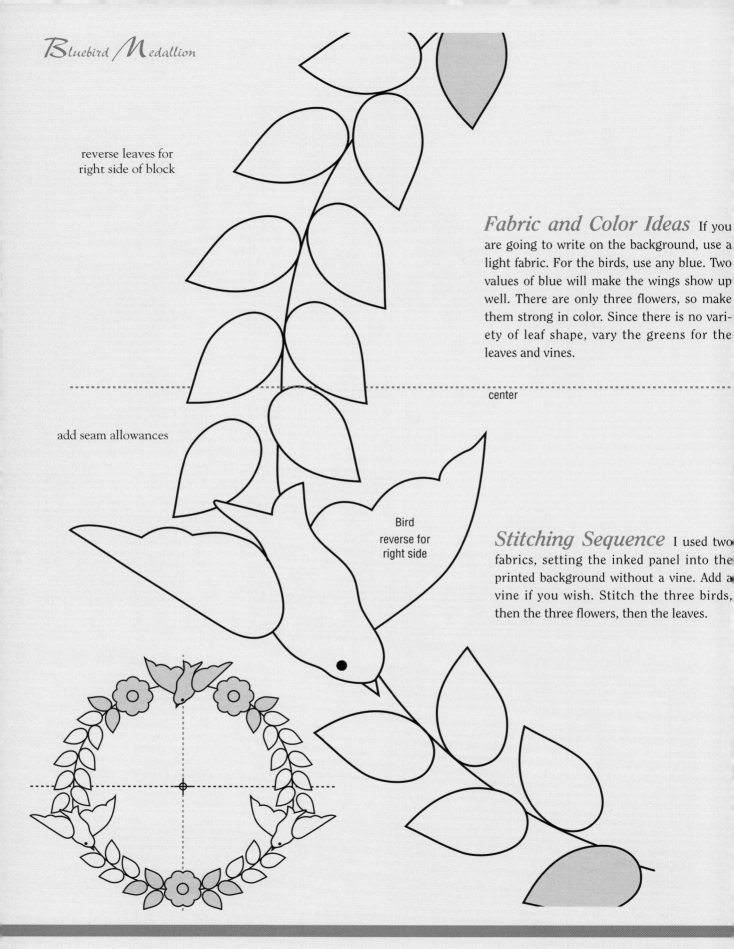

reverse leaves for
right side of block

Fabric and Color Ideas If you
are going to write on the background, use a
light fabric. For the birds, use any blue. Two
values of blue will make the wings show up
well. There are only three flowers, so make
them strong in color. Since there is no variety of leaf shape, vary the greens for the
leaves and vines.

center

add seam allowances

Bird
reverse for
right side

Stitching Sequence I used two
fabrics, setting the inked panel into the
printed background without a vine. Add a
vine if you wish. Stitch the three birds,
then the three flowers, then the leaves.

center

center

add seam allowances

Design dimensions: 12" x 9"
Block size: 16" x 12"
Finished quilt size: 24" x 20"

Spring Pussy Willow

Border Design The scalloped edge is often seen on traditional antique quilts. In this small and softly colored quilt, the light blue border is divided from the center only by the scalloped edge. The cool lime green scallops do not contrast with the blues of the center and border; rather, they blend gently, providing a cool transition from one to the other

Design Considerations

The two unusual features of this block are the inked branches of the pussy willow and the embroidery technique used to make the pussy willow buds realistic. The inked branches look realistic with their craggy turns and subtle shading and give the design a pictorial feeling. The multi-thread embroidery technique, developed by Marguerite Shattuck, makes the pussy willow buds show-stoppers and is worth imitating. The scalloped edge is made with Susan's Simple Borders Ruler. The outer border is 4 inches wide.

Fabric and Color Ideas

For the background use a pale, sky-like fabric, and a darker value of blue for the border. The scallop is a medium value chartreuse green. The pussy willow buds are made of a medium gray solid while the leaves use dark greens in a solid or printed fabric. Use an orange or peach, hand-dyed or equivalent, for the bird bellies and a blue directional print or hand-dyed look for the bird bodies and wings. For pussy willow buds, use gray fabric and three shades of gray embroidery floss. For legs, use brown; for beaks, use yellow; and for eyes, use black.

Inking Process

❑ Ink the branches before sewing. To achieve the painted watercolor effect, mix several pens together. (I used the Fabrico yellow and light green, and the Pigma green and brown. Practice this technique on a scrap of fabric. Playing with just one branch will show you how easy it is.

❑ Lay the fabric over the pattern and trace the branches in yellow. Fill them in completely with the yellow. The joy of this technique is that it doesn't matter how precise you are—things can stick out or get wider and it just looks more realistic.

❑ With the green pen, cover and shade some of the yellow. Irregularity and sketchiness is your goal. It doesn't matter where or how much—try shading about half or one side only of the branches. Check out the shading techniques on pages 31-33. Work from the outside line of the branch to the inside. You can always add more. You will be delighted to see how even this little bit of green enhances the depth of the branches.

❑ Use the brown Pigma pen to outline one side of all of the branches. Notice that I outlined most of the branches, making the left side wider and visually stronger and drawing a narrow, almost undetectable line on the right side. Use a sketchy, uneven stroke, so the brown fades into the background colors and doesn't look like solid color.

add seam allowances

connect here

Fancy Feathered Friends – *Susan McKelvey*

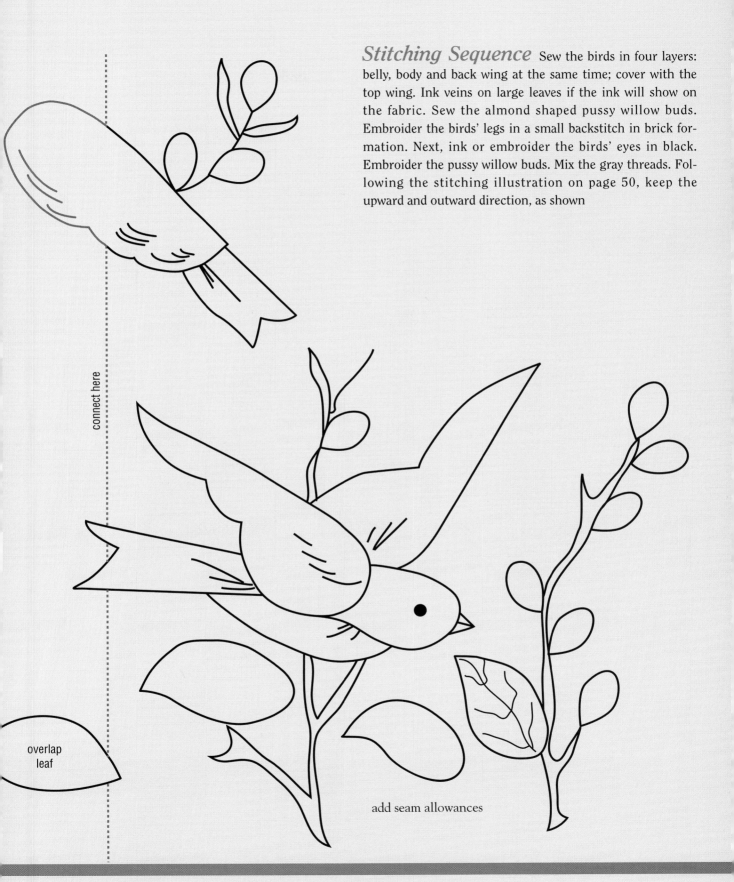

Stitching Sequence Sew the birds in four layers: belly, body and back wing at the same time; cover with the top wing. Ink veins on large leaves if the ink will show on the fabric. Sew the almond shaped pussy willow buds. Embroider the birds' legs in a small backstitch in brick formation. Next, ink or embroider the birds' eyes in black. Embroider the pussy willow buds. Mix the gray threads. Following the stitching illustration on page 50, keep the upward and outward direction, as shown

connect here

overlap leaf

add seam allowances

I desire no future
that will break
the ties of the past
George Eliot

Design dimensions: 10" x 10"
Block size: 13" x 13"
Finished quilt size: 22" x 22"

Wedding Bouquet

Fancy Feathered Friends – *Susan McKelvey*

Fabric and Color Ideas A delicate overall print in slate blue was used for the background. For the flowers, leaves, birds, and pie crust border, use rich and variegated hand-dyed fabrics. For the branches, brown or green fabrics work best. Repeat the blue in the border fabric.

Stitching Sequence Cut the background and press a fold through the center in both directions. Ink the center space first with your verse. Next add the branches, birds, flowers and leaves.

add seam allowances

fold

Fancy Feathered Friends – Susan McKelvey

Cheery Cherry Time

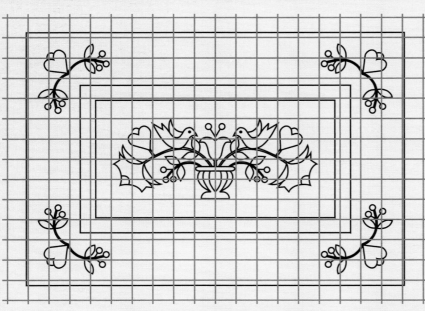

Design dimensions: 20" x 8"
Block size: 23" x 12"
Finished quilt size: 36" x 25"

Each square equals 2 inches.

Fancy Feathered Friends – *Susan McKelvey*

add seam allowances

reverse

Ⓐ

Fabric and Color Ideas Because the color scheme is simple, add interest where you can with big or elaborate prints. I chose a bright white background. For the birds use any blue you like; I chose two prints of pure blue. Use several reds with gold accents for the flowers, vase and hearts, and several greens for the leaves. The outer border repeats the background from the center. Appliqued hearts, stems and cherries repeat the elements in the corners. A red and green stripe, cut on the bias, adds movement as well as pulling out the reds from the center.

add seam allowances

Design for border corners
(Refer to layout grid
on page 54.)

connect Ⓐ here

Stitching Sequence Sew the stems to define the position of other elements. Stitch the center flower to cover the stem. Place the vase to cover the vines and flower stems. Next come the large outer flowers and leaves. Add the birds, hearts and cherries. Embroider the tiny stems. In the border corners: stems, heart, cherries, leaves (all repeated from the center).

Design dimensions: 10" x 10"
Block size: 18" x 15"
Finished quilt size: 34" x 27"

Arbor Feast

add seam allowances

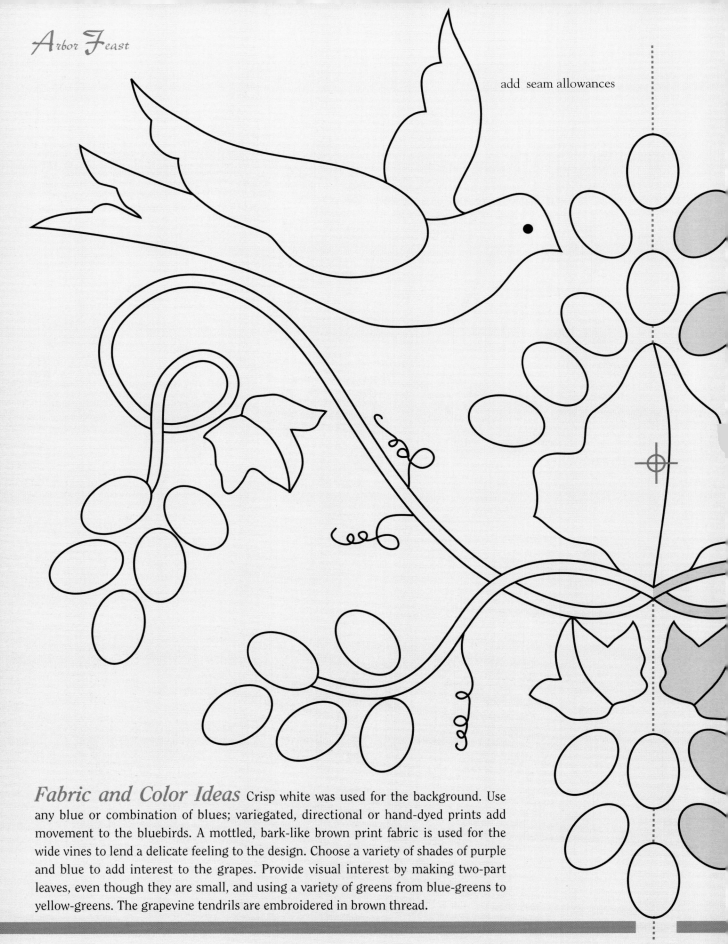

Fabric and Color Ideas Crisp white was used for the background. Use any blue or combination of blues; variegated, directional or hand-dyed prints add movement to the bluebirds. A mottled, bark-like brown print fabric is used for the wide vines to lend a delicate feeling to the design. Choose a variety of shades of purple and blue to add interest to the grapes. Provide visual interest by making two-part leaves, even though they are small, and using a variety of greens from blue-greens to yellow-greens. The grapevine tendrils are embroidered in brown thread.

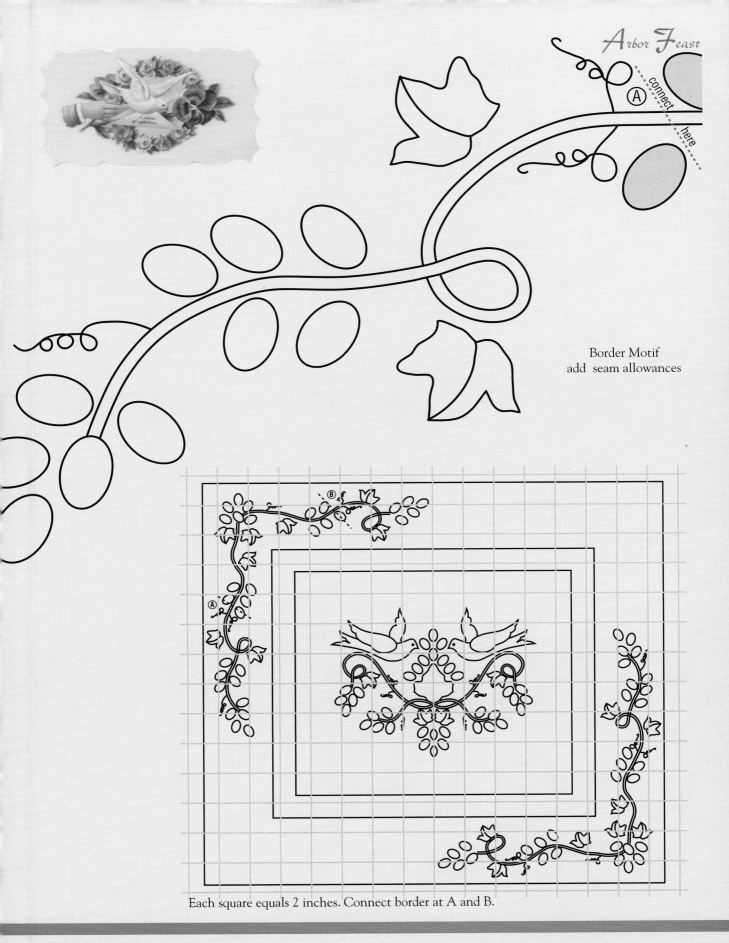

A connect here

Border Motif
add seam allowances

B

A

Each square equals 2 inches. Connect border at A and B.

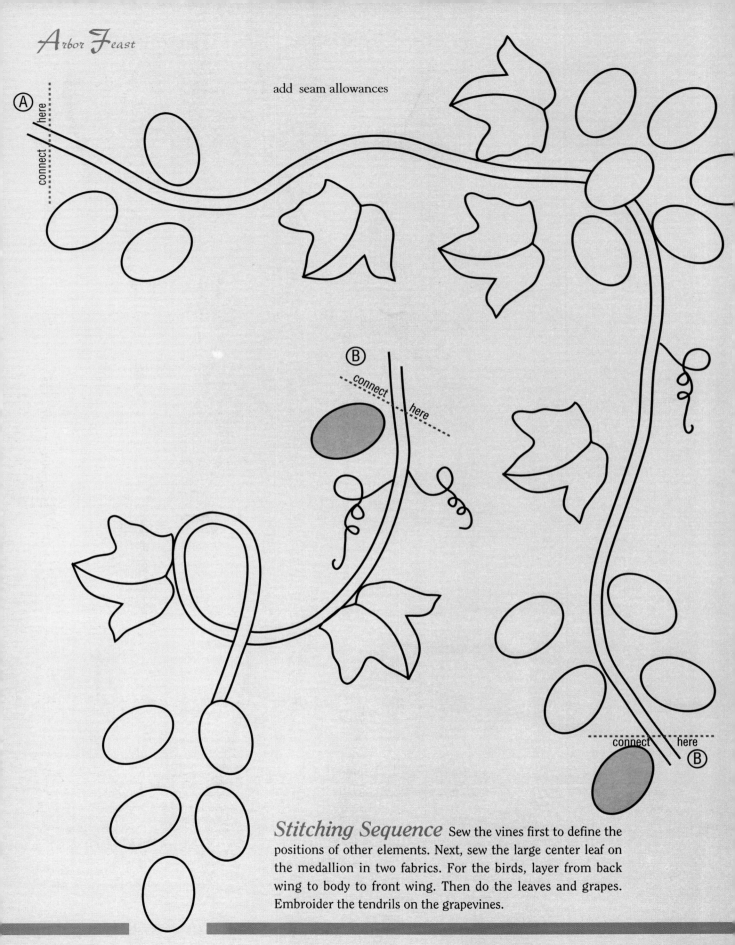

add seam allowances

Ⓐ connect here

Ⓑ connect here

Ⓑ connect here

Stitching Sequence

Sew the vines first to define the positions of other elements. Next, sew the large center leaf on the medallion in two fabrics. For the birds, layer from back wing to body to front wing. Then do the leaves and grapes. Embroider the tendrils on the grapevines.

Intermediate Projects

AMID THE ROSES

AMID THE HOLLY

Fabric and Color Ideas

A delicate beige on white floral print provides texture in the background. For all the elements, I used variegated fabrics, which give texture. Inking provides more shading on the petals and birds' tummies and defines veins on the leaves. The birds' eyes and beaks are embroidered. The pansy centers contain yellow French knots. The blue and green floral print on the dogtooth border edges adds richness as it echoes the blue of the birds. For more information on edging borders with appliqué, refer to page 37

Stitching Sequence

Sew the birds in place. Work downward from the birds as you layer the leaves and flowers. For the berries on AMID THE HOLLY, I found I had to adjust the berries–sometimes adding more or moving or enlarging them them slightly to fill space. Ink and embroider the details. Shade the rose petals from the outside in matching colors. Shade the pansy centers lightly outward from the center in black. Add veins to the leaves in green or brown, and dot the birds' eyes in brown or black. Embroider the birds' beaks and the pansy centers with yellow thread and any tiny stems in green.

Design dimensions: 7¼" x 9"
Block size: 14½" x 14½"
Finished quilt size: 25" x 25"

Amid the Pansies

Fancy Feathered Friends – *Susan McKelvey*

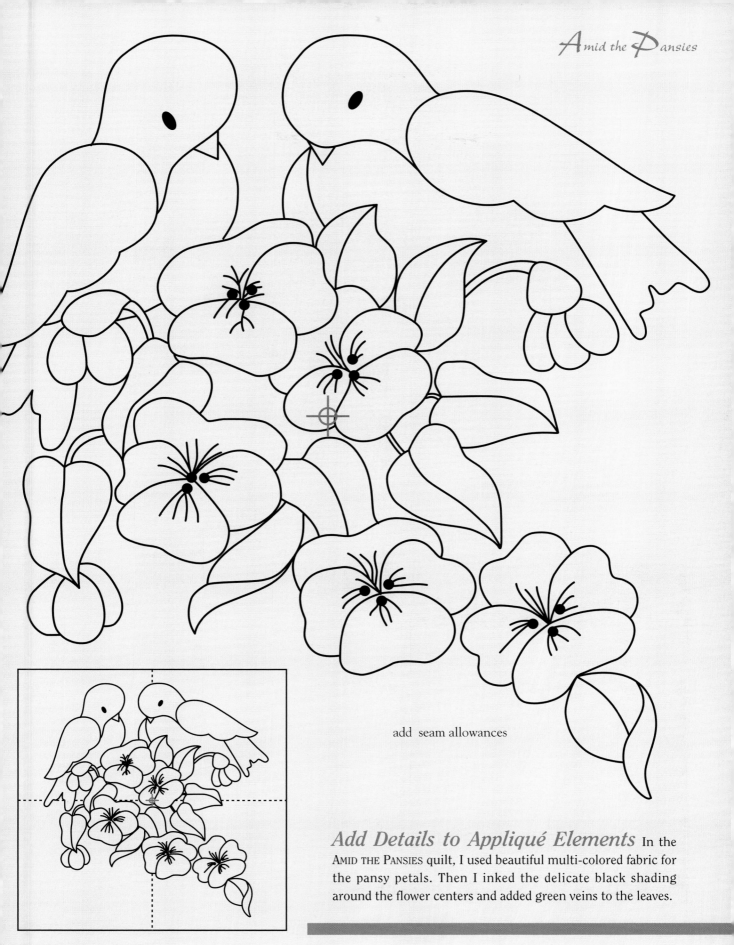

add seam allowances

Add Details to Appliqué Elements In the
AMID THE PANSIES quilt, I used beautiful multi-colored fabric for
the pansy petals. Then I inked the delicate black shading
around the flower centers and added green veins to the leaves.

Design dimensions: 7¼" x 9"
Block size: 14½" x 14½"
Finished quilt size: 25" x 25"

A mid the Roses

add seam allowances

Design dimensions: 7¼" x 9"
Block size: 14½" x 14½"
Finished quilt size: 25" x 25"

*A*mid
the
*H*olly

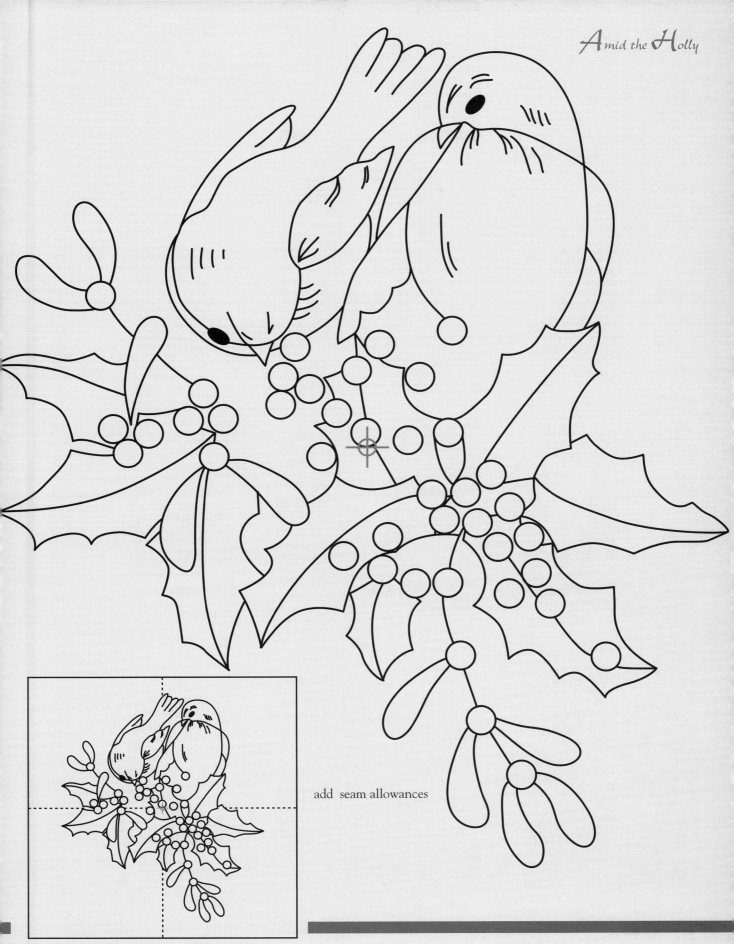

add seam allowances

Design dimensions: 21" x 20"
Block size: 20½" x 18½"
Finished quilt size: 30½" x 28½"

Huddled on a Garden Wall

Fancy Feathered Friends – *Susan McKelvey*

Each square equals 2 inches.

add seam allowances

Fabric and Color Ideas Any sky-like fabric
would be lovely (cut 23" x 10"). For the brick wall (23" x
12"), I chose a brown hand-dyed fabric and drew the bricks
with a brown Identipen™ (any large pointed pen would do).
Ink the fabric before sewing the quilt top. Use a cement-looking print, mottled
beiges, for the top of the wall (23" x 1½"). Use any shaded blues and peaches for
the birds. The pattern shows you where to shade the feathers. Do this by tracing *before* you sew. White petals, yellow centers, all shaded with yellow and
brown pens, are perfect for the daisies (see page 32). Use several greens for the
leaves and steam. Leaf veins are shaded with green ink.

Stitching Sequence Piece the sky, ledge and wall to make the back-
ground. Mark the middle. Add the flower stems, then the flowers and leaves.
Appliqué the birds 1 inch left of center; place the lone bird with wing tip 4
inches right of center or wherever he looks right to you.

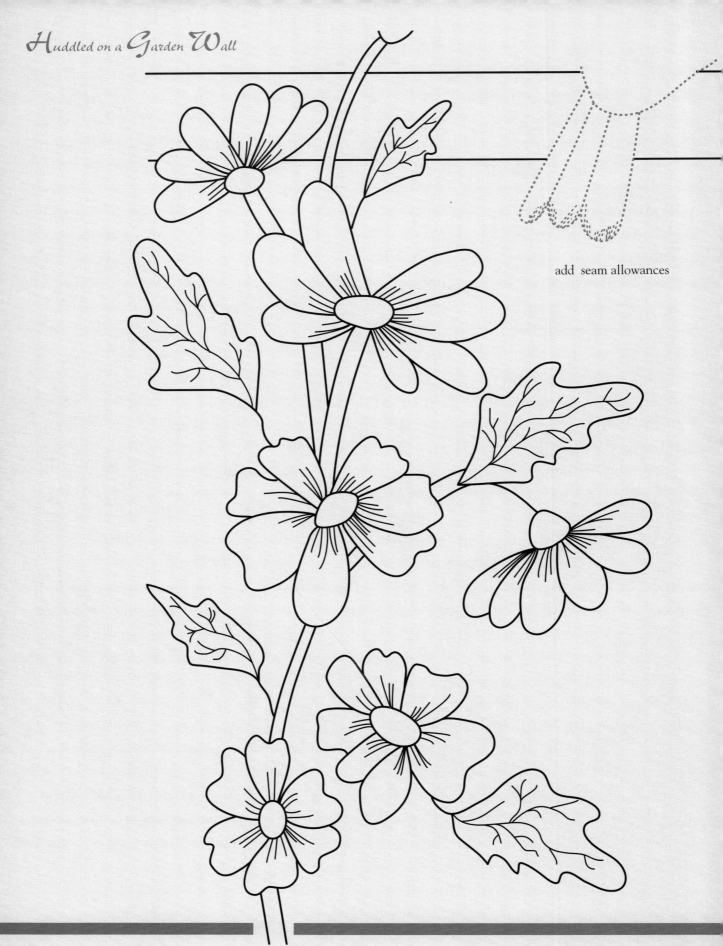

add seam allowances

Fancy Feathered Friends – *Susan McKelvey*

bird in background

inking diagram
for brick wall

top →

Design dimensions: 20" x 20"
Block size: 22" x 22"
Finished quilt size: 41" x 41"

Oh, What a Lovely Meal!

Fabric and Color Ideas

The maroon plaid, while beautiful and rich, creates color problems because it is so strong. Choose colors for the elements that will stand out on this background. I chose a bright turquoise for the birds.

Use varied and bright, fun prints in warm orange, yellow, red, fuschia and purple for the grapes, flowers and leaves. The vase must be strong enough to show but recede enough to let the grapes and flowers dominate. Use a variety of green fabrics in chartreuse and other brights for the leaves and vines. The colors from the center are echoed in the multiple borders.

Stitching Sequence Place the vase in the center and then the birds. Embroider the vines. Place the flowers, grapes, and leaves last. These can be adjusted around the vines and birds.

Each square equals 2 inches.

Advanced Projects

SWIRLING BLUEBIRDS

DESCENDING DOVES

PRETTY PAPERCUT

VASE OF POMEGRANATES

May flowers
of Love
Around thee
be twined,
And the sunshine
of peace
Shed its joy
o're thy mind.
— Antique Valentine

Design dimensions: 12" x 14"
Block size: 18½" x 17¾"
Finished quilt size: 28" x 27"

Descending Doves

Ⓐ connect here

Each square equals 2 inches.

Fabric and Color Ideas For the
background use a marbled sky-like blue. Choose
any blue you like for the birds. For the wings, try
a multi-colored marbled fabric. Several variegated
yellow/pinks and pink/reds can be used for the
roses and buds. Use a variety of green fabrics for
the leaves and vines. Linda Tonyes used Ultra-
suede™ for the tiny leaves.

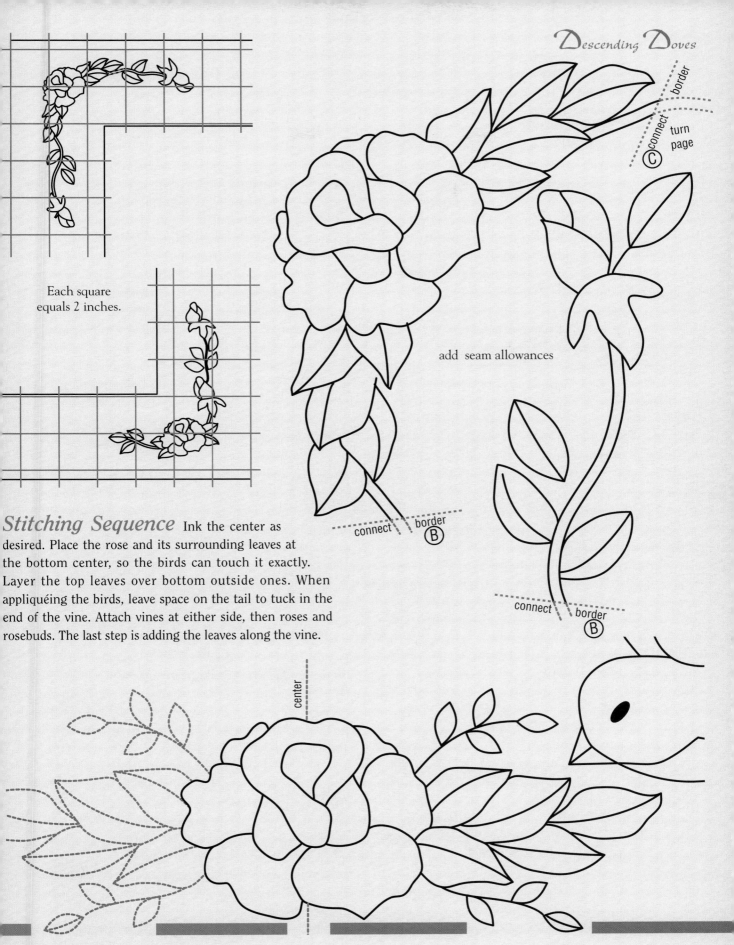

Each square equals 2 inches.

border

Cconnect

turn page

add seam allowances

connect border ⒷB

connect border ⒷB

Stitching Sequence Ink the center as desired. Place the rose and its surrounding leaves at the bottom center, so the birds can touch it exactly. Layer the top leaves over bottom outside ones. When appliquéing the birds, leave space on the tail to tuck in the end of the vine. Attach vines at either side, then roses and rosebuds. The last step is adding the leaves along the vine.

center

Fancy Feathered Friends – Susan McKelvey

Descending Doves

turn
page ©
connect border

add seam allowances

Detail of shaded rosebud.

connect here
Ⓐ

bottom border

Design dimensions: 13" x 13"
Block size: 15" x 15"
Finished quilt size: 55½" x 55½"

Swirling
Bluebirds

BB

center

BB

BBr

Fabric and Color Ideas For

birds, use any blue or combinations of blues
like; variegated, directional or commer
hand-dyes add movement. Fabrics that cr
realism should be used for the floral sprays.
at least three greens, or as many as you wish
the leaves. Browns and tans are natural cc
for the acorns. Use varied greens or leaf p
for the ivy and reds for the cherries.

center

add seam allowances

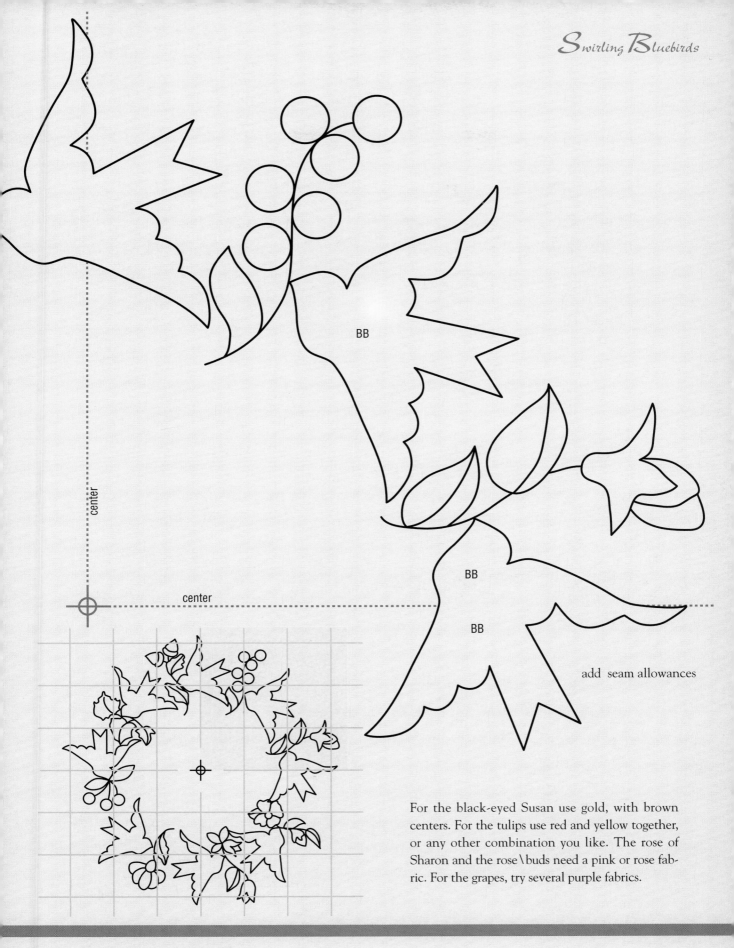

center

center

BB

BB

BB

add seam allowances

For the black-eyed Susan use gold, with brown centers. For the tulips use red and yellow together, or any other combination you like. The rose of Sharon and the rose\buds need a pink or rose fabric. For the grapes, try several purple fabrics.

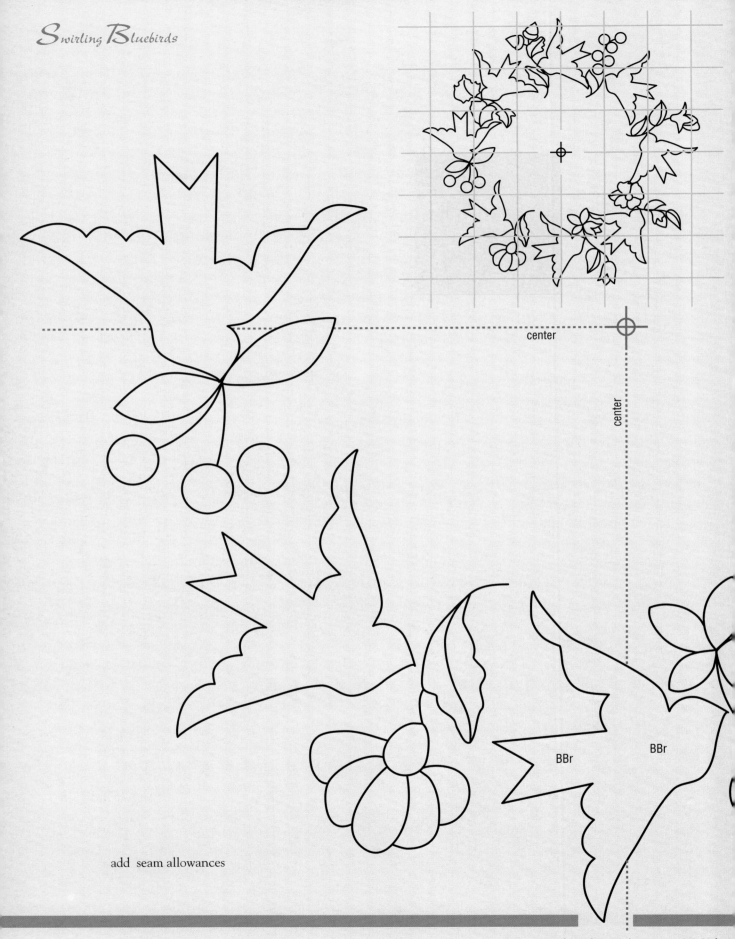

center

center

BBr

BBr

add seam allowances

center

center

BB

BBr

BBr

add seam allowances

Design dimensions: 16" x 9"
Block size: 21¼" x 13½"
Finished quilt size: 32¾" x 25¾"

Vase of Pomegranates

Fancy Feathered Friends – *Susan McKelvey*

add seam allowances

Fabric and Color Ideas The dark green vines allow the birds and flowers to take center stage. The leaves, in a variety of strong green folk prints, balance the bright birds. The pair of major leaves feature two values of green accented with gold check. Three values of red provide richness for the pomegranates. The seeds, "fussy-cut" from tiny paisleys, add detail.

add seam allowances

Each square equals 2 inches.

Stitching Sequence

Sew in this order: stem, center pomegranate, vase, and two major leaves. The layered detailing on each leaf can be done before sewing it onto the background fabric. Sew the two birds next, followed by the two side pomegranates. Adjust the vines around the birds' backs. Attach the leaves.

Border Design

At the border corners, sew the vines, pomegranates, and leaves. Echo the appliqué elements in the border corners. A huge border might overwhelm a small wall quilt, or simply be too much work. Try repeating some key design elements from the quilt center in the four border corners, or in two opposite corners. This takes very little time, yet carries the design from the quilt center toward the corners of the quilt.

Although traditional in style, this VASE OF POMEGRANATES quilt design seems light-hearted and yearns for a gay, folk border treatment. The yellow background fabric sets the tone, and the bright, pure colors in the appliqué elements create a cheerful atmosphere. The narrow inner border echoes color from the center appliqué motifs, and the outer border repeats the appliqué elements themselves. The pomegranate is so striking that it is the logical choice for the four corners, and the vines and leaves extend the design as they wrap around the sides. The blue binding again echoes the blue of the birds, major elements that needed repeating.

Design dimensions: 26" x 26" point to point
Block size: 31" x 31"
Finished quilt size: 42½" x 42½"

Pretty Papercut

Fabric and Color Ideas Because the color scheme is simple, add interest with a large scale or elaborate print and a lovely border. The pie crust hearts could also be used as border elements

Stitching Sequence

❑ Cut the background fabric 36" x 36". Make your pattern from freezer paper. Iron it onto a 30" x 30" square of appliqué fabric to mark the sewing lines. Mark the sewing lines with a fine-pointed permanent pen (a Pigma .01 works well). You will be sewing for a long time, and this guarantees that the lines will be there when you need them.

❑ Remove the freezer paper pattern, but keep it nearby in a plastic bag while you sew. You may need it to refresh your sense of where you are on the design. Cut out the appliqué element, leaving several inches of fabric outside the marked design. Don't cut any of the center areas.

❑ Mark the center with a safety pin. Anchor the large medallion onto the background fabric, using lots of safety pins to keep it in position.

❑ Sew around the outer edges of the medallion first. This anchors it and guarantees its correct positioning on the background fabric. Cut a seam allowance ahead of yourself as you need to, but only cut as far as you can stitch in a single sitting. That way, there will never be any fraying around the very tiny seam allowances. Remove the safety pins as you sew, so they will not get in the way.

❑ After you sew the entire outer edge, begin stitching the inner side of the heart. Lift, slit, and cut the medallion as you go, using tiny scissors and great care. Then pin well. Stitch around the hearts scallops.

Border Design
This detailed papercut or Scherensnitte design needed to be the undisputed focal point of this Pretty Papercut quilt, so a simple border treatment was called for. The simple red-and-white color scheme is pure nineteenth century in feeling, and always a dramatic choice. The border print, which looks like two striped fabrics, is actually a single print. The double crosshatch quilting is another echo of bygone days.

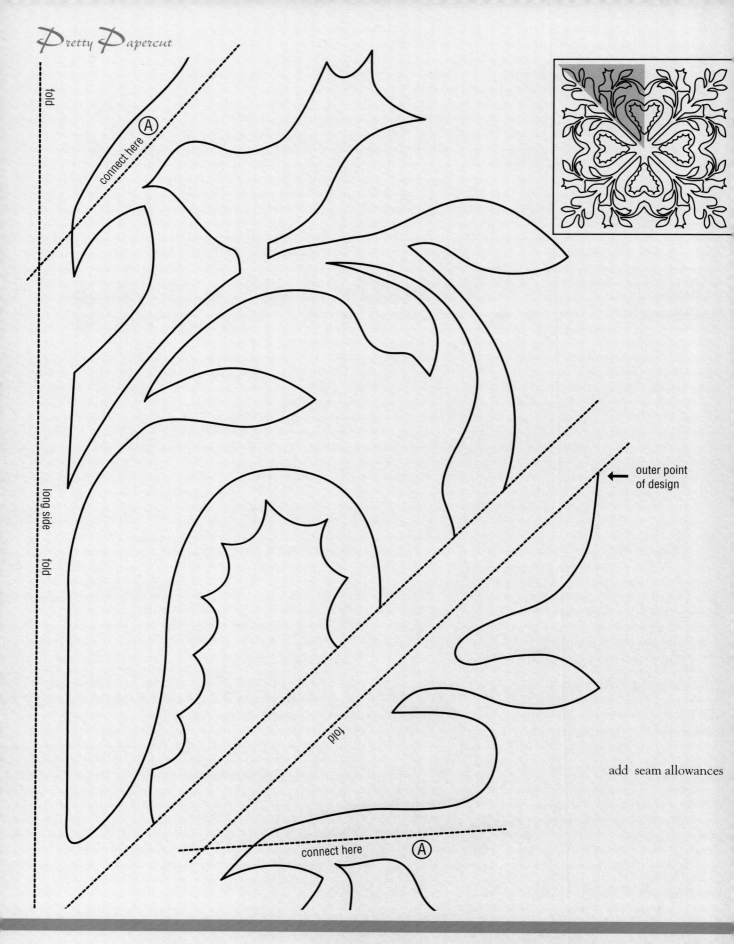

fold

connect here Ⓐ

long side   fold

outer point
of design

fold

add seam allowances

connect here   Ⓐ

Finished quilt size: 60" x 60", block sizes 10" x 10". Designed by Susan McKelvey; blocks made by Susan and friends. Top row: An Elegant Pair, Yum Yum Tree, Vineyard Feast. Middle row: Love Birds, Vase of Plenty, Hovering Birds. Bottom row: Roosting Amid the Cherries, A Bouquet to Oneself, Cherry Pickers

Birds of Old

Border Design

These nine BIRDS OF OLD blocks were inspired by blocks found on a variety of antique quilts from the mid-nineteenth century, and were made to go together in a traditional quilt set. Here I used red and green on a white background, a color scheme typical of 1850s Baltimore quilts. To enhance this period feeling, I set the blocks with simple red sashing and added a wide, white inner border with a double red dogtooth edge. The outer border print acts as a simple red frame for the detailed blocks in the center of the quilt.

Block Fabric and Color Ideas

For the birds, choose at least two contrasting blues and a yellow. The trees and branches can be one or two browns, and the leaves and possibly some branches in a variety of greens. Use one or two reds and one or two golds for the flowers. The acorn needs two brown shades. Several values of purple, blue and fuschia will do nicely for the grapes. Use brown embroidery floss to match the brown fabric on the tiny stems. Use Ultrasuede™ and silk embroidery for the tiniest elements.

Stitching Sequence

Cut the stem 3 inches longer than needed. Stitch the stem, but leave some fabric hanging free, so you can tuck it into the seam later. Stitch the calyxes next, followed by the flowers and buds. The large leaves can be two-part leaves. Stitch the birds. Add the small leaves. Stitch the acorn. Ink or embroider the eyes and beaks.

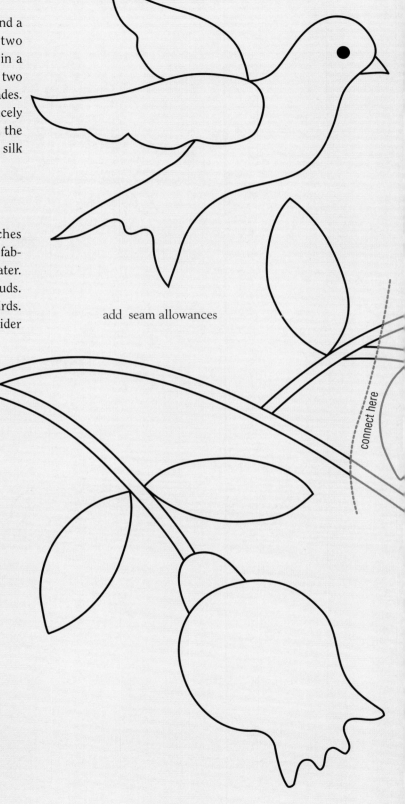

add seam allowances

connect here

Block 1: An Elegant Pair

Fancy Feathered Friends – *Susan McKelvey*

add seam allowances

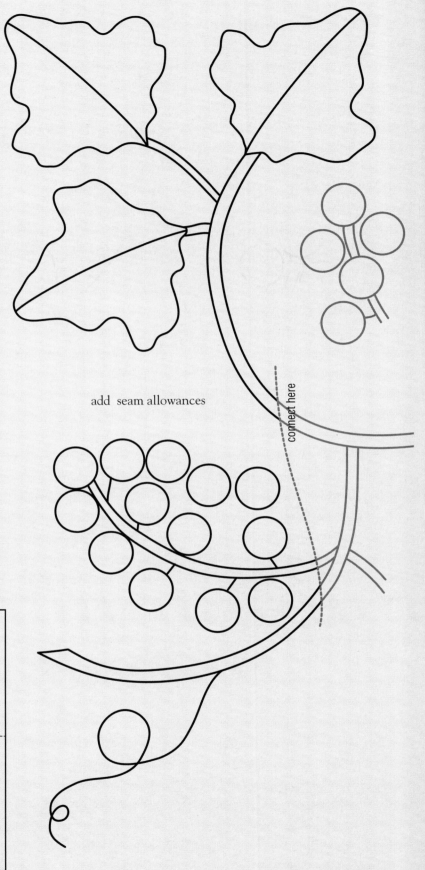

Stitching Sequence Sew the stems and the leaves that cover the stem ends. Stitch the bird in three layers. Add the grapes. Embroider or ink the grapevine tendrils in brown. Ink the bird's eye or embroider one French knot.

add seam allowances

connect here

Block 3: Vineyard Feast

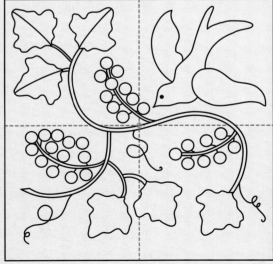

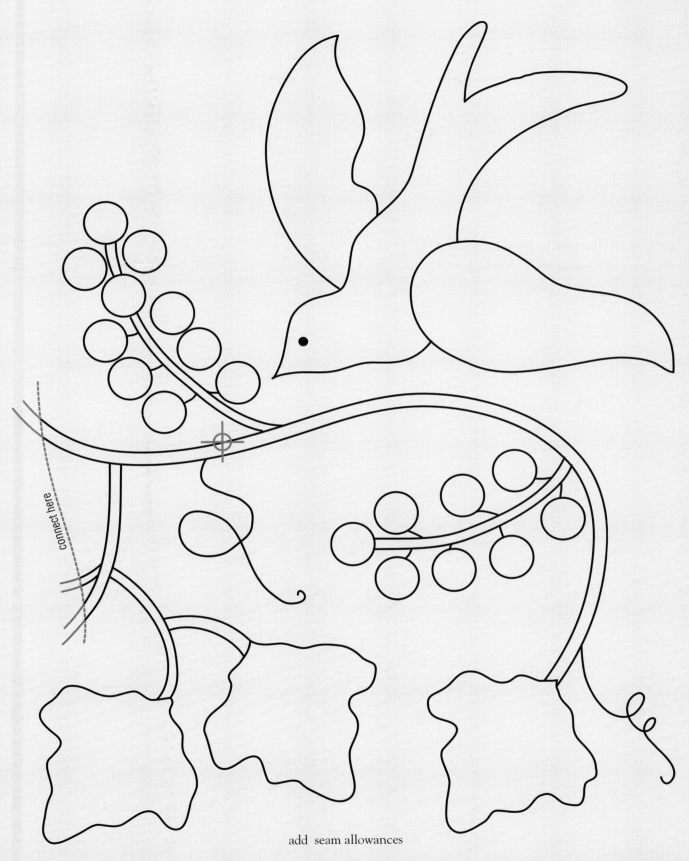

connect here

add seam allowances

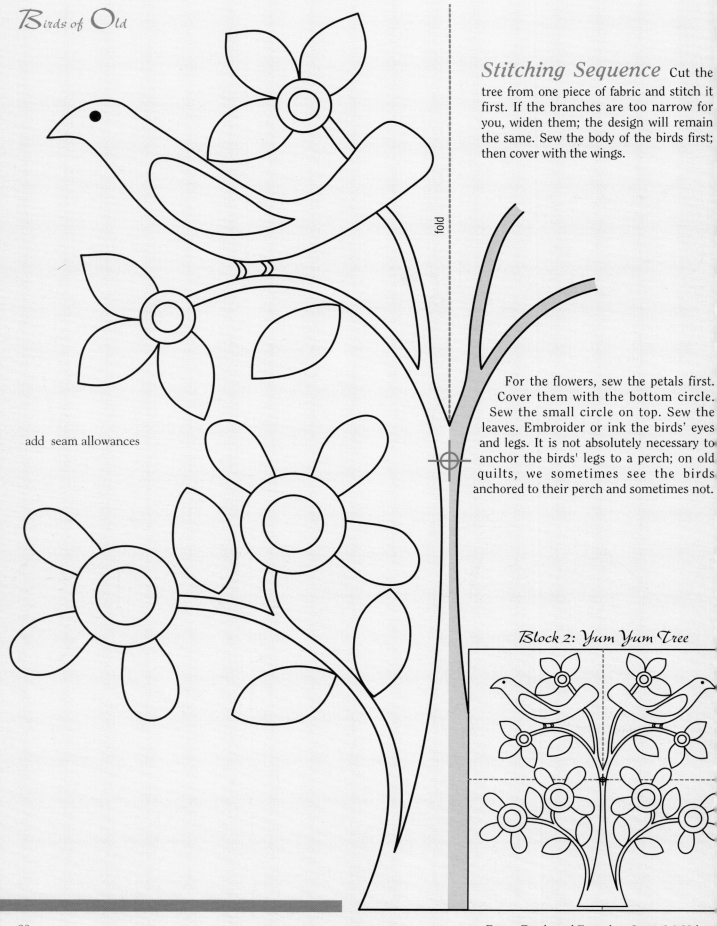

Stitching Sequence Cut the
tree from one piece of fabric and stitch it
first. If the branches are too narrow for
you, widen them; the design will remain
the same. Sew the body of the birds first;
then cover with the wings.

fold

For the flowers, sew the petals first.
Cover them with the bottom circle.
Sew the small circle on top. Sew the
leaves. Embroider or ink the birds' eyes
and legs. It is not absolutely necessary to
anchor the birds' legs to a perch; on old
quilts, we sometimes see the birds
anchored to their perch and sometimes not.

add seam allowances

Block 2: Yum Yum Tree

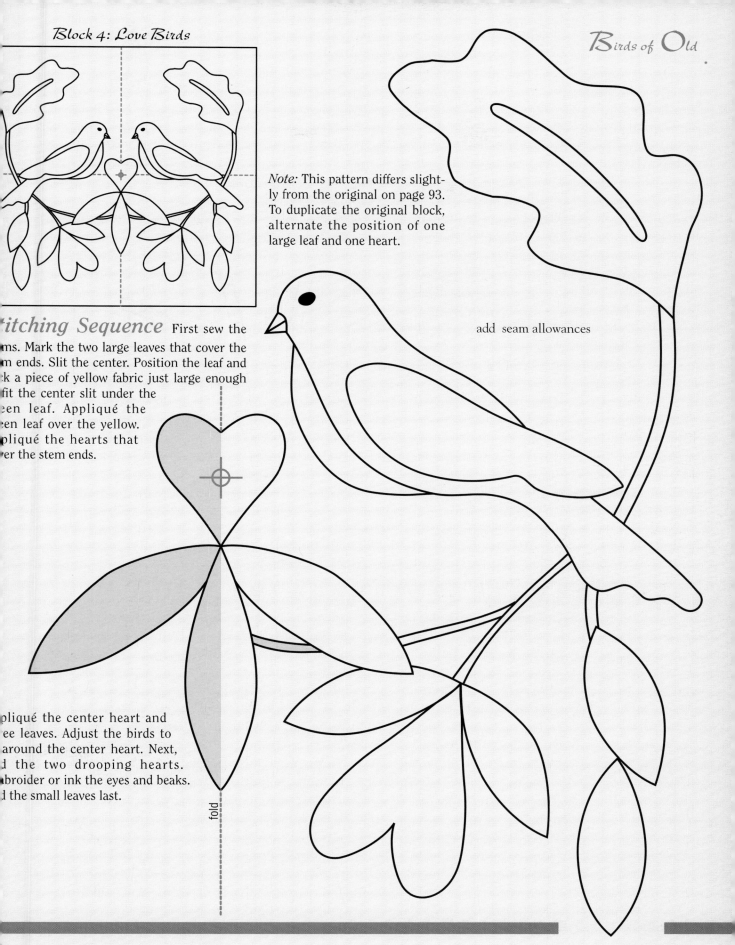

Note: This pattern differs slightly from the original on page 93. To duplicate the original block, alternate the position of one large leaf and one heart.

add seam allowances

itching Sequence First sew the
ms. Mark the two large leaves that cover the
m ends. Slit the center. Position the leaf and
k a piece of yellow fabric just large enough
fit the center slit under the
en leaf. Appliqué the
en leaf over the yellow.
pliqué the hearts that
er the stem ends.

pliqué the center heart and
ee leaves. Adjust the birds to
around the center heart. Next,
l the two drooping hearts.
broider or ink the eyes and beaks.
l the small leaves last.

fold

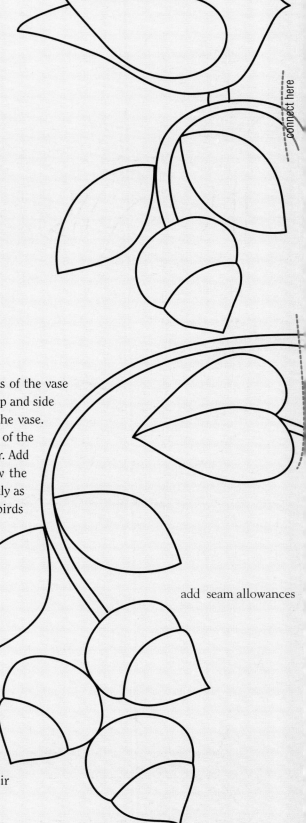

add seam allowances

VASE OF PLENTY, *by Eleanor Eckman, 32″ x 32″.*

Stitching Sequence

Stitch the branches first. Sew the parts of the vase together, appliqué the gold dogtooth edge onto the vase body, leaving top and side seam allowances open. Appliqué the gold piece across the bottom of the vase. Appliqué the vase onto the background, leaving space to insert the tops of the handles. Add the handles. Stitch the center flower. Add the flower center. Add the acorns. Sew the two-part leaves on the two sides of the vase. Sew the leaves on the center branch. Add the small leaves, adjusting them slightly as needed, but keeping the placement on both sides identical. Attach the birds in two parts. Add the tiny flowers and leaves. Embroider them in silk ribbon if desired. Ultrasuede™ works well, too. Finally, embroider or ink the tiny stems in green or brown thread.

Border Design

This design has enough detail and presence to stand alone as a wall quilt. The narrow inner border has two useful features: it picks up several of the colors from the center design and, because the stripe is at an angle, it provides movement around this highly balanced quilt. I frequently make the sashing out of stripes on the diagonal because they add an element of surprise to a traditional set. The border repeats two major elements from the center: the acorns and the single red center flower. Because the center design and its red flower are perfectly balanced, I repeated this balance in the border. The red flowers are centered on each edge, the acorns fill the corners, and the vines with their leaves meander around the entire quilt.

connect here

connect here

add seam allowances

repeat bird her

ad
flow

add seam allowances

Block 6: Hovering Birds

fold

Fancy Feathered Friends – *Susan McKelvey*

Stitching Sequence For Hovering Birds, cut the tree from one piece of brown fabric and sew it first. If the branches are too narrow for you, widen them; the design will remain the same. Sew the vase to cover the tree base. For the large flowers, sew the three parts of the flower together before appliquéing the unit to the background fabric. Sew the center plume. Sew the birds in three layers. Add the leaves and tiny flowers. The ones in the quilt are made of Ultrasuede™. Embroider or ink the tiny stems and the birds' eyes and beaks.

Stitching Sequence For Roosting Amid the Cherries, cut the tree from one piece of brown fabric and sew it first. If the branches are too narrow for you, widen them; the design will remain the same. Sew the birds in two steps. Sew the leaves in place. Embroider the cherry stems in brown or green thread. Add the cherries. Ink or embroider the birds' eyes and beaks.

connect here

connect here

add seam allowances

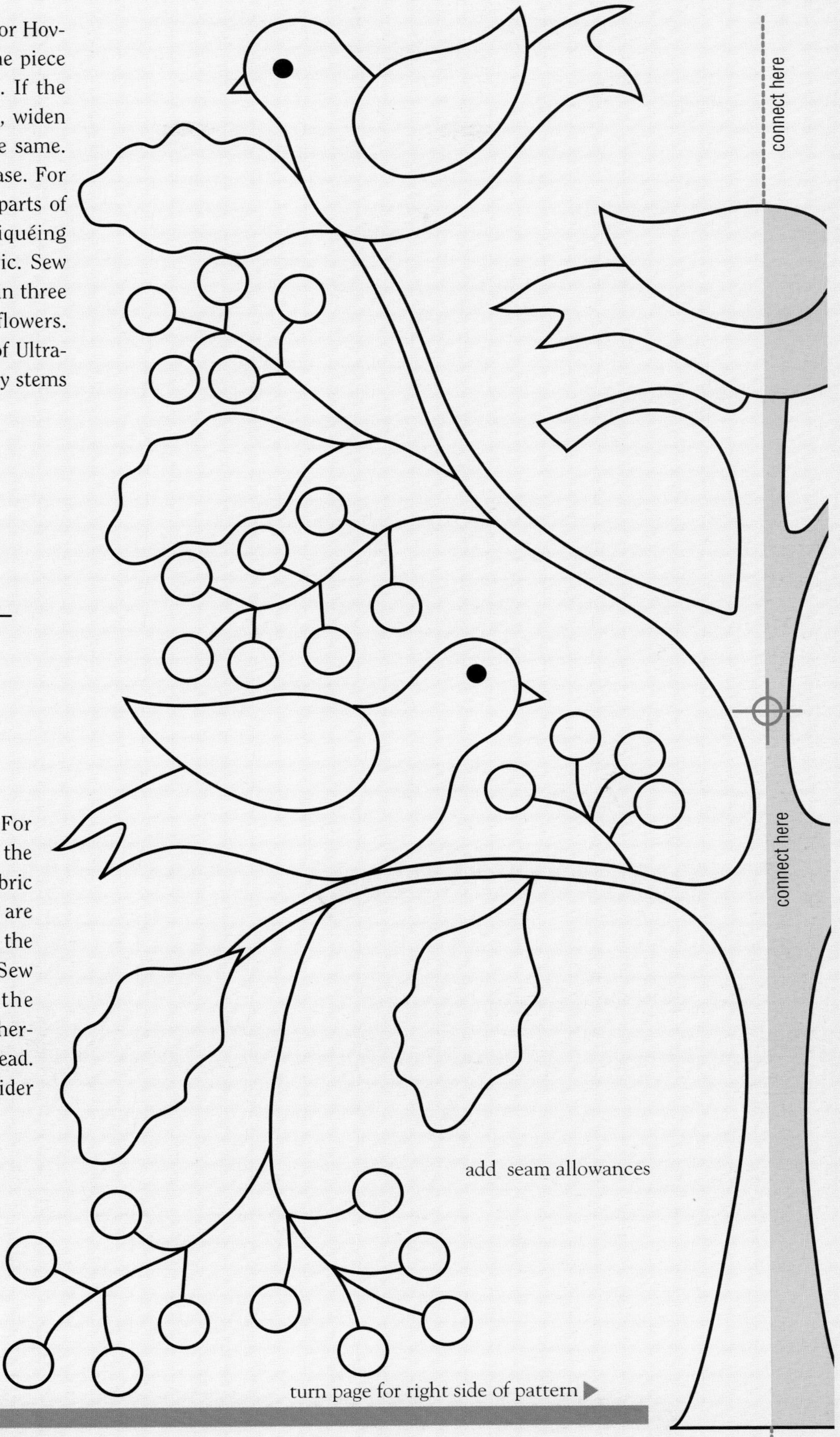

turn page for right side of pattern ▶

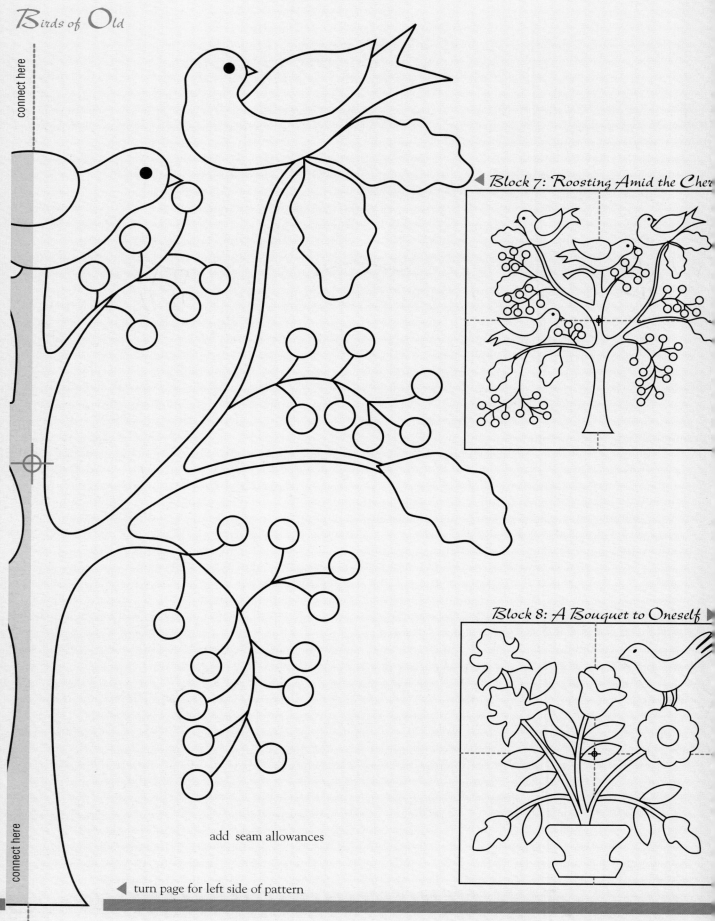

Block 7: *Roosting Amid the Cher*

Block 8: *A Bouquet to Oneself* ▶

add seam allowances

connect here

◀ turn page for left side of pattern

Stitching Sequence Stitch the stems first; then stitch the flower pot to cover the stem ends. Add the flowers to cover the stem tops.

ct here

add seam allowances

Leaves Use a variety of greens for the leaves. Simplify the bird's tail if you want—two or three scallops rather than the deep inside points. Embroider or ink the bird's legs.

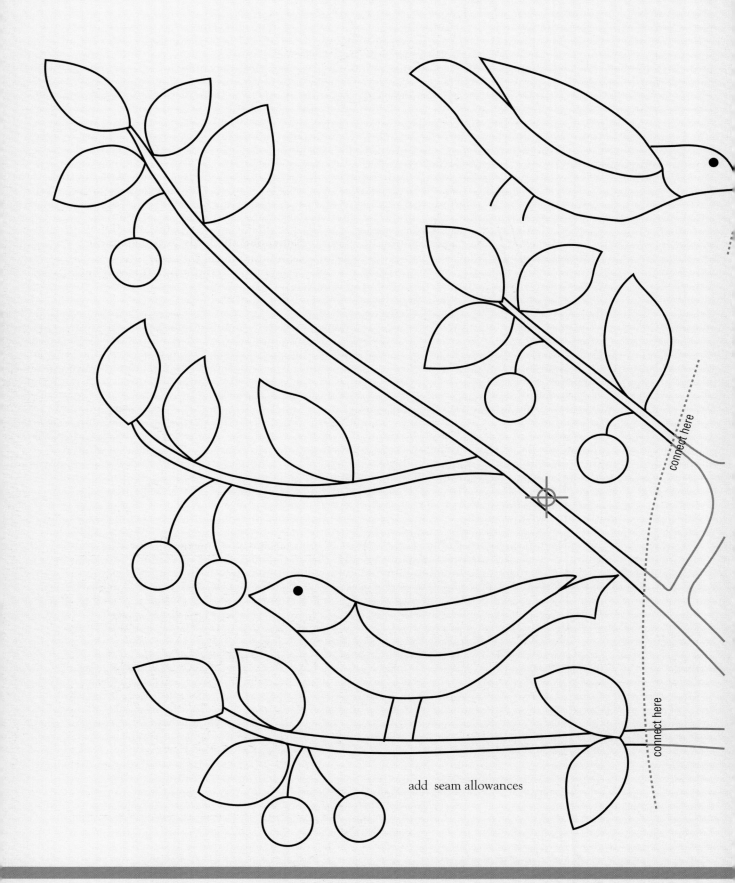

connect here

connect here

add seam allowances

Fancy Feathered Friends – *Susan McKelvey*

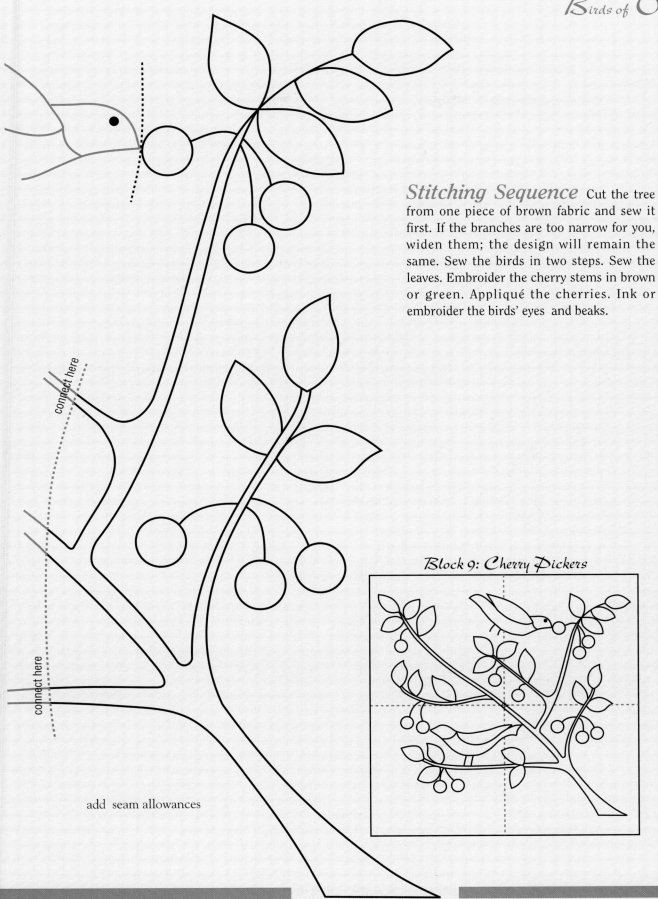

Stitching Sequence Cut the tree from one piece of brown fabric and sew it first. If the branches are too narrow for you, widen them; the design will remain the same. Sew the birds in two steps. Sew the leaves. Embroider the cherry stems in brown or green. Appliqué the cherries. Ink or embroider the birds' eyes and beaks.

connect here

connect here

connect here

Block 9: Cherry Pickers

add seam allowances

The Quiltmakers

LESLIE'S WEDDING QUILT, 67" x 67", made by Susan McKelvey for her daughter, Leslie McKelvey Adelman; quilted by Eileen Schamel

My grateful thanks to the quiltmakers who appliquéd and quilted for me. Without their help, I could not have included so many wonderful quilts in this book. When I sent out the call for help in making quilts, I had no idea what kind of response to expect, the generosity these women would show, or the beautiful gifts they would create from my ideas. I received offers of help from all over the country, and these volunteers truly made this book. Without their input and efforts, the quilts would lack variety and sensitivity. They gave of their time, energy, and talent without asking for reward. Although every quilt was not finally included, the contributions of the quiltmakers were no less important. This, then, is their book, too.

The **Quiltmakers**

Anita Askins of Annapolis, Maryland, appliquéd one SONGBIRD ON A BASKET block.

Rolinda Collinson of Friendship, Maryland, appliquéd BARN SWALLOWS.

Eleanor Eckman of Lutherville, Maryland, appliquéd and quilted the wall quilt VASE OF PLENTY, and quilted AMID THE PANSIES.

Fran Gillesheimer of Whiting, New Jersey, appliquéd two BIRDS ON BANNERS blocks.

Judi Gunter of Severna Park, Maryland, appliquéd one SONGBIRD ON A BASKET block.

Leslie Heilman of Purcellville, Virginia, appliquéd one BIRDS ON BANNERS block and one SWIRLING BLUEBIRDS block and quilted WEDDING BOUQUET.

Lynn Irwin of Sparks, Maryland, appliquéd one SWIRLING BLUEBIRDS block.

Ann N. Kelsey of Londoner Heights, Maryland, appliquéd OH, WHAT A LOVELY MEAL!

Diane Keull of Glenn Dale, Maryland, appliquéd one SWIRLING BLUEBIRDS block.

Marjorie Mahoney made PRETTY PAPERCUT and appliquéd BLUEBIRD WREATH.

Dori L. Mayer of Eldersburg, Maryland, appliquéd one SWIRLING BLUEBIRDS block and quilted HUDDLED ON A GARDEN WALL.

Jane McCabe of Sheboygan Falls, Wisconsin, made VASE OF POMEGRANATES.

Berta Murray of University Park, Maryland, appliquéd a SONGBIRD ON A BASKET block and Vineyard Feast for BIRDS OF OLD. She also quilted AMID THE ROSES.

Joy Nichols of Portland, Oregon, made ARBOR FEAST and appliquéd two BIRDS ON BANNERS blocks.

Lynn Phillips of Abingdon, Maryland, appliquéd Yum Yum Tree for the BIRDS OF OLD quilt.

Barbara Rasch of White Hall, Maryland, appliquéd one Songbird on a Basket, and Love Birds for BIRDS OF OLD. She also quilted SPRING PUSSY WILLOW.

Marguerite Shattuck of Fresno, California, made CHEERY CHERRY TIME and appliquéd and embroidered SPRING PUSSY WILLOW.

Georgina Shultz of Annapolis, Maryland, quilted OH, WHAT A LOVELY MEAL! and appliquéd Cherry Pickers for the BIRDS OF OLD quilt.

Linda Tonyes of Philadelphia, Pennsylvania, appliquéd DESCENDING DOVES, two BIRDS ON BANNERS blocks, the Vase of Plenty block for BIRDS OF OLD and one block for SWIRLING BLUEBIRDS.

Mary Tozer of Elko, Nevada, appliquéd Hovering Birds for BIRDS OF OLD.

Ruth Warren of Harrington, Delaware, appliquéd two BIRDS ON BANNERS blocks and one SWIRLING BLUEBIRDS block.

Cynthia Whyte of Adamstown, Maryland, appliquéd An Elegant Pair for BIRDS OF OLD and one block for SWIRLING BLUEBIRDS.

Pat Wood of Centerville, Maryland, appliquéd Roosting Amid Cherries for the BIRDS OF OLD quilt.

Resources

Fabric pens, signature stamps, Susan's Simple Appliqué Borders Ruler, books and patterns on writing, tracing and appliqué, Susan's Bluebirds of Happiness fabric for Benartex

Books and Supplies for Writing and Drawing on Fabric

Wallflower Designs by Susan McKelvey
27680 Goldsborough Neck Road
Easton, MD 21601
susanmckelvey.com

Fabric pens and Painting Supplies

Jukebox
P. O. Box 1518
Tustin, CA 92781-1518
jukeboxquilts.com

Fabrics

Susan McKelvey's Fabrics
Benartex, Inc.
1359 Broadway
New York, NY 10018
1-800-benartex • www.benartex.com

Bibliography

Bishop, Robert. *New Discoveries in American Quilts.* New York: E.P. Dutton & Co., Inc., 1975.

Bowman, Doris M. *The Smithsonian Treasury: American Quilts.* Washington, D.C.: Smithsonian Institute Press., 1991.

Brackman, Barbara. *Encyclopedia of Appliqué.* McLean, Virginia: EPM Publications, Inc., 1993.

Brackman, Barbara and Jennie A. Chin Sara Davis, Farley Reimer, Nancy Hornback, Farley and Terry Thompson. *Kansas Quilts & Quilters.* Lawrence, Kansas: The University Press of Kansas, 1993.

Duke, Dennis and Deborah Harding. *America's Glorious Quilts.* New York: Park Lane, 1987.

Katzenberg, Dena. *Baltimore Album Quilts.* Baltimore: The Baltimore Museum of Art, 1981.

Kiracofe, Roderick. *The American Quilt.* New York: Clarkson Potter, 1993.

Seaman-Allen, Gloria and Nancy Gibson-Tuckhorn. *A Maryland Album.* Nashville: Rutledge Hill Press, 1995.

Warren, Elizabeth T. and Sharon L. Eisenstat. *Glorious American Quilts.* New York: Penguin Studio, 1996.

Zegart, Terri. *Quilts: An American Heritage.* New York: SMITHMARK, 1994.

McKelvey, Susan. *A Treasury of Quilt Labels.* Lafayette, CA: C&T Publishing, 1993.

_____. *Color for Quilters II.* Millersville, Maryland: Wallflower Designs, 1993.

_____. *Friendship's Offering.* Lafayette, CA: C&T Publishing, 1987.

_____. *Light & Shadows.* Lafayette, CA: C&T Publishing, 1989.

_____. *Limitless Labels to Trace.* Millersville, Maryland: Wallflower Designs, 1996.

_____. *More Scrolls & Banners to Trace.* Millersville, Maryland: Wallflower Designs, 1992.

_____. *Scrolls & Banners to Trace.* Millersville, MD: Wallflower Designs, 1990.

_____. *Traceables from Baltimore Album Quilts at the Maryland Historical Society.* Millersville, Maryland: Wallflower Designs, 1994.

McKelvey, Susan and Pepper Cory. *The Signature Quilt.* Saddle Brook, NJ: Quilt House Publishing, 1995.

About the Author

Susan McKelvey caught the quilting bug in 1977 in a quilting class in Greensboro, North Carolina. The first assignment was to stitch one Dresden Plate block. Susan was so excited that she made twenty, used up all of her scraps, and found herself hooked. Although quilting was not a part of her family heritage, it has become a part of her children's lives–they grew up under her design and sewing tables.

In 1984, Susan wrote her first quilt book, *Color for Quilters*, and many have followed. Susan has indulged her passion for quilts and fabric as an artist, author, designer, and entrepreneur. Through her company, Wallflower Designs, she has produced many patterns and tools for quilters.

Susan earned a B.A. in English from Cornell College in Mt. Vernon, Iowa, and an M.A. in English from the University of Chicago. She taught English at the secondary level for many years, including a two-year tour in Ethiopia with the Peace Corps. Today, with children grown, Susan and her husband live on Maryland's rural Eastern Shore near the Chesapeake Bay. She currently divides her time between quilting, gardening, and volunteering for golden retriever rescue. The family's cats and rescued goldens divide their time between dreaming on Susan's many quilts and helping to calm the many foster dogs who pass through the McKelvey home–leading Susan to ponder, "Why is it that all of these animals, fosters included, believe they were born to grace quilts?"

Other AQS Books

This is only a small selection of the books available from the American Quilter's Society. AQS books are known worldwide for timely topics, clear writing, beautiful color photos, and accurate illustrations and patterns. The following books are available from your local bookseller, quilt shop, or public library.

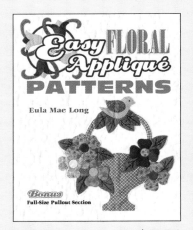

#6300   us$24.95

#6077   us$24.95

#6292   us$24.95

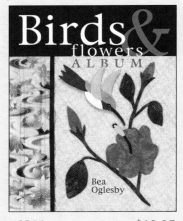

#6211   us$19.95

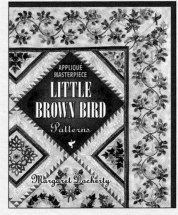

#6303   us$29.95

#6208   us$24.95

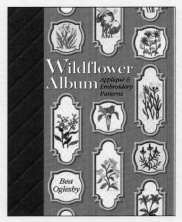

#5757   us$19.95

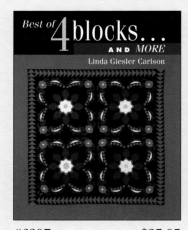

#6297   us$25.95

#5335   us$21.95

LOOK for these books nationally. CALL or VISIT our website at www.AQSquilt.com

1-800-626-5420